Published by OR Books in collaboration with Little Broad Studio, New York and London

Visit our website: **www.orbooks.com**

First printing 2023

Library of Congress Cataloging-in-Publication Data: A catalog record for this book is available from the Library of Congress. British Library Cataloging-in-Publication Data: A catalog record for this book is available from the British Library.

ISBN 978-1-68219-421-8

The Other Almanac

Established in 2022

Co-Published between Little Broad Studio and OR Books

ISBN 978-1-68219-421-8

Editor-in-chief: **Ana Ratner**

Editing: **robin herold**

Cover Illustration: **Daniel Barreto**

Layout and Design: **Kayley Sonheim**

Editorial Support: **Sam Silver**

Astrologer: **Morgan Lett**

Data Visualization: **Jing Jing Wang**

https://otheralmanac.com

@almanac.other

The Other Almanac

For city and country and everywhere in between

CALCULATED FOR THE YEAR

2024

FOR THE MERIDIAN OF NEW YORK, NY

40.7128° N, 74.0060° W

Volume 2

Knowledge Acknowledgment

The Other Almanac would like to call out and acknowledge conventional American almanacs' history of theft of the knowledge, research, and philosophies developed and refined by the people of many distinct Native nations. Much of the information contained in these almanacs would not exist without Native peoples' ongoing collaboration with the ecosystems, flora, and fauna of this land over thousands of years.

Often in land acknowledgements gratitude for stewardship and knowledge is given. As a settler on stolen land, I question the appropriateness of giving thanks for land and knowledge forcibly taken and misused, rather than given with trust. *The Other Almanac* aspires to navigate those contradictions with care and to embody solidarity with colonized and oppressed peoples everywhere, from New York to Palestine, between and beyond.

I am unabashedly grateful that most of humanity's years on earth were lived before European colonialism and the invention of capitalism. I am thankful that this planet and everything it supports has been stewarded and respected for much longer than it has been wounded and depleted.

If you are reading this publication in the so-called United States of America, you are standing, sitting, or lying down on stolen land, violently transformed by systematic strategies of erasure, including genocide, ecocide, and intentional transmission of disease.

The Other Almanac strives to be a platform for the work of many people(s), including artists and writers of Indigenous descent from around the world. While I take pride in this second publication, I know we can continue to do better. As future editions are published, we look forward to expanding the depth of our commitment to sharing the work of people who themselves or their ancestors were displaced or wounded through colonization.

The Other Almanac contributes funds monthly to the Indigenous Environmental Network. All non-Native readers are encouraged to find out which nation's land they are currently occupying and to pay a monthly land tax to organizations in their area.

—Ana Ratner

Whose land are you on?

https://native-land.ca

Below is a list of a few organizations to look into.

https://indigenousrising.org

https://ienearth.org

https://mannahattafund.org

https://therednation.org

https://nativefoodalliance.org

https://sogoreate-landtrust.org

About Almanacs

The Other Almanac is a contemporary reimagining of the much-beloved farmers' almanacs. There have been many different almanacs throughout the last couple hundred years, with *The Old Farmer's Almanac* being the most widely known, as well as the longest continuous printed publication in the United States.

If *The Other Almanac* is your introduction to the incredible history of almanacs here in the US and the world, then welcome to a very deep new study. You are now taking part in one of the oldest cultural and scientific traditions of humanity.

The first printed almanac was created in Europe in 1457, but almanacs have existed across the globe for much longer, since the discipline of astronomy came into being. They were carved into stones, painted on animal hides, and formed into manuscripts. The oldest surviving almanac was found in Babylonia and lists each day of the year with corresponding favorable and unfavorable activities.

Yearly updated almanacs are still being printed in many countries around the world. *The Other Almanac* is calculated and written for New York State (hopefully expanding geographically in coming years). Unlike other almanacs in the US, which have historically catered to rural white farmers and land-owners, *The Other Almanac* attempts to be a bridge between the rural and urban divide here in the USA. This edition is a second attempt at an almanac that talks about climate change, takes stances on cultural and political issues, and includes contributions from professors, farmworkers, scientists, medicine makers, incarcerated poets, activists, astrologers, urban gardeners, midwives, and more. This project is a huge undertaking and I look forward to seeing it grow and change as it continues throughout the years.

Thank you to everyone who helped bring this publication into existence. Many eyes, hands, machines, and minds went into creating this object and I hope you enjoy reading it as much as we enjoyed making it.

—*Little Broad Studio*

Contents

DATA

New York Native Seeds...12
Most Common Tree Species NYC...14
Hourly Wages in U.S. Prisons..22
Phone Call Rate in U.S. Prisons...23
Honey Industry Production..24
Plant Flowering Times in New York...26
Climate and Seasonal Data..28

OBITUARIES

Fauna Extinction Obituaries...16
Flora Extinction Obituaries..18
Tech Extinction Obituaries - Sally Dewind...20

CALENDARS

Moon Calendar 30
Full Year Calendar...32
January Calendar..34
February Calendar..46
March Calendar...56
April Calendar...66
May Calendar..74
June Calenda...86
July Calendar...96
August Calendar..104
September Calendar..112
October Calendar..122
November Calendar 130
December Calendar...140

MOON NAMES

Moon Names...34, 46, 56, 66, 74, 86, 96, 104, 112, 122, 130, 140

MONTHLY COLUMNS

The Other Wardrobe - Chloë Boxer...36, 59, 89, 114
Phenology Calendar - Kay Kasparhauser.........37, 49, 59, 77, 88, 99, 106, 115, 125, 133 ,143
Astrology - Morgan Lett.............................38, 48, 58, 68, 76, 89, 98, 106, 115, 125, 133, 143
Herbal Tips - Veladya Chapman..................38, 49, 58, 69, 77, 88, 99, 106, 114, 124, 133, 143

RECIPES

Soup Joumou - Food With Fam + Andrew Ceneus...40
Haitian Legume - Food With Fam + Andrew Ceneus...64
Haitian Griot & Pikliz - Food With Fam + Andrew Ceneus..90
Haitian Black Rice - Food With Fam + Andrew Ceneus..116

PROSE

44, What Feels True - adrienne maree brown...42
Black Feminist Lessons From Marine Mammals - Alexis Pauline Gumbs....................50
The Disappearance - Carla J. Simmons..60
Water: Between Life and Greed - Yaku Pérez Guartambel..70
Alligator Mama - Lily Consuelo Saporta Tagiuri...78
An Era of Romanticism on Social Media - Andrea Aliseda..92
Rerooting - Kirk Gordon..100
Red Water - Dylan Smith...108
On Recognition Technologies - Sophia Giovannitti...118
Third Act - Bill McKibben..126
Edenic Time - Jessie Kindig...134
Reflections on the Modern Dialectics of Preservation and Erasure - Jumana Manna.....138
The Mall - Philip Poon...144

POETRY

The Liberation of the Chinook Wind - Tania Willard...53, 54

Blood Is Always Red - Jennifer Givhan...110

ART

Monthly Flash Tattoo - Who Tattoo 39, 48, 58, 68, 76, 88, 98, 107, 115, 124, 132, 142

What Haunts Us/What Heals Us - Amaryllis R. Flowers..44

Not Alone - Bread and Puppet Press...62

Be Afraid of The Enormity of the Possible - Alfredo Jaar...72

Meissen Pump + - Francesca DiMattio...82

Pump III - Francesca DiMattio...84

Body Builder Deities in the Garden - Esther Elia...95

Boombox - 10th Floor Studio..102

Carrizo Mountain Dance - Tyrrell Tapaha..111

Sunflower - Keegan Dakkar Lomanto..119

Weightlifter3 - Hannah Beerman...120

Untitled (Blue and Gold) - Dyani White Hawk..128

The Shadow of Night Makes Way for Morning Light - Chris Lloyd.............................136

Mehmana/Guests - Hangama Amiri...148

RESOURCES

Mutual Aid Groups of New York...154

Community Gardens of New York 150

Community Fridges..153

Apothecaries/Botanicas/Wellness Centers from The Database of Black Healers and
Herbalists - compiled by Jade Forrest Marks..155

CONTRIBUTOR BIOS

Contributor Bios...156

IMAGE INDEX

Image Index...159

HIBISCUS MOSCHEUTOS,
SWAMP ROSE MALLOW

AQUILEGIA CANADENSIS,
RED COLUMBINE

CHELONE GLABRA,
WHITE TURTLEHEAD

IMPATIENS PALLIDA,
YELLOW JEWELWEED

PHYSOCARPUS OPULIFOLIUS,
NINEBARK

PYCNANTHEMUM MUTICUM,
MOUNTAIN MINT

SENNA HEBECARPA,
WILD SENNA

LILIUM CANADENSE,
CANADA LILY

CEANOTHUS AMERICANUS,
NEW JERSEY TEA

THUJA OCCIDENTALIS,
ARBORVITAE

SMILAX HERBACEA,
SMOOTH CARRIONFLOWER

AUREOLARIA PEDICULARIA,
**THE FERNLEAF YELLOW
FALSE FOXGLOVE**

NEW YORK
NATIVE SEEDS

13

Top 10 Most Common Tree Species in NYC

Ginkgo	Silver Maple	Red Maple	Green Ash	Tillia Cordata	Pin Oak
2.8%	3.2%	3.5%	3.5%	4.7%	7.5%

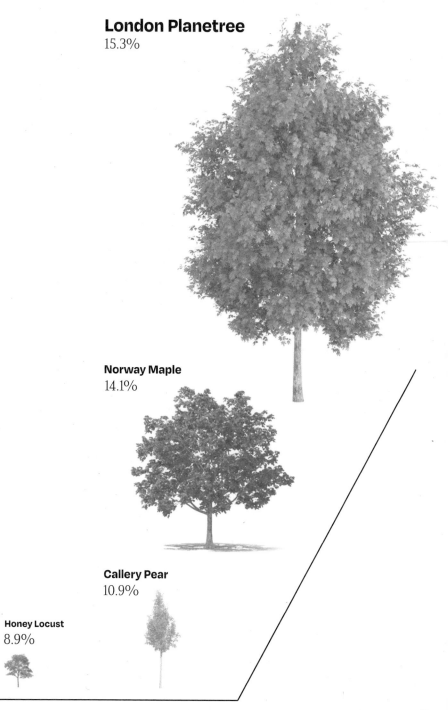

London Planetree
15.3%

Norway Maple
14.1%

Callery Pear
10.9%

Honey Locust
8.9%

FAUNA

Extinction Obituaries *2021-2022*

In 2022 (the IUCN Red List has not been updated for 2023) we officially lost 66 species, mostly due to conditions created by us humans. Although some of the species we highlight died out years ago, *The Other Almanac* follows the lead of the Red List and goes by the date the extinction was published. Due to this discrepancy in timing, the images we use are most often of related species, not the species eulogized.

An expanded version of some of the following obituaries first appeared in *The Nation*.

YANGTZE STURGEON OR DABRY'S STURGEON | ACIPENSER DABRYANU
Declared extinct in the wild | 2022

For almost 30 million years the Yangtze Sturgeon enjoyed a quiet life in the depths of the Yangtze river, vacuuming small fish, crustaceans, molluscs, and aquatic insect larvae into their prehistoric mouths. So, it is with profound sadness that we announce that on July 21, 2022, the Yangtze Sturgeon, watery companions to shad, carp, and a muddy assortment of other bottom dwellers, was declared extinct in the wild.

Our sturgeon friends grew slowly, and each one could have outlived every member of the 27 Club by a few years. For sturgeon they were considered small, but the loss of their comparatively unimposing bodies weighs heavy on our hearts.

We humans overfished them because we thought they tasted delicious, and we loved eating their imported eggs from tiny silver spoons or on top of little toasts. We also dumped polluted waste water around them when we built developments and removed forests along the banks of their home. We wish we could say that was all we did, but we also built electric dams that blocked their migration.

While we eventually woke up to their travails, and tried to save them by instituting a fishing ban and reintroducing some of their captive-bred brethren into the Yangtze, we wish we had cared enough to do more even sooner. We really do miss seeing them making their way back and forth along the river.

MARACAY HARLEQUIN FROG
ATELOPUS VOGLI
Declared extinct | 2022

We would love to tell you that the last Maracay Harlequin Frog died peacefully in its home in Maracay, Venezuela, but that wouldn't be very honest of us. We don't imagine that having one's habitat destroyed and turned into a bustling city would be a peaceful way to go. While the poison in our beloved frogs' skin protected them from the jaws of predators, it seems it couldn't keep them safe from our appetite for deforestation.

On quiet days we like to imagine that we can still hear the Maracay Harlequin Frog's call, a low vibrating buzz, coming down from the great semi-deciduous forest of the heavens. Or perhaps it's just a cellphone. Whatever it is, and wherever our amphibian friends are now, we hope that their long toes are climbing the tallest trees, and that the ants and mites taste better than they ever did on earth. There will be no funeral. In lieu of flowers, please honor their memory by suppressing your urge for habitat destruction.

MAURITIUS DUCK | ANAS THEODORI
Declared extinct | 2022

We don't usually condone gravedigging, but in the case of the Mauritius Duck we are glad that their fossilized remains were uncovered 129 years ago in Mare aux Songes on the island of Mauritius.

We wish we knew more about this duck-of-many-names time on Earth, but sadly the written records we have of them are not sufficient to know their likes and dislikes or their hearts' deep desires. We know they were dabbling ducks who frequented the freshwater marshes and ponds on the islands they called home. We also know that, until the Dutch arrived in 1598, the ecosystem where our endemic friends flapped and waded had remained undisturbed by humans in any significant way.

Enough time has passed that we would hope the Mauritius Duck could forgive us for what we did, but since we haven't yet learned from our mistakes we don't expect to be granted that pardon any time soon. For now, all we can say is that we are sorry we hunted them to extinction, killed their bird friends, and demolished their home as swiftly as Elon Musk demolished Twitter.

FLORA

Extinction Obituaries *2022-2023*

ESCARPMENT CYCAD
ENCEPHALARTOS BREVIFOLIOLATUS
Declared extinct in the wild | 2022

It is with deep sadness that we inform you that the Escarpment Cycad, a member of the zamiaceae family whose ancestors survived three mass extinctions, is no longer with us. It has gone the way of the sauropod, which was known to munch happily on cycad leaves until a 110-mile-wide asteroid plunged into the earth. While our hardy cycad friend was able to survive what the sauropod could not, it did not, alas, manage to outlast us humans.

Although Escarpment Cycads had been around longer than opposable thumbs, there were only five to seven of them left when we humans first learned about their existence in 1995. After they were discovered, poachers dug up most of them to sell for thousands of dollars to private collectors. The loss of a species that few will have heard of, and even fewer seen, may not seem noteworthy. But, if you've ever seen a painting, drawing, or a movie with a dinosaur, they or their cousins are almost always there, in the background, fronds bristling, looking like slightly confused palm trees.

While we would like to blame the Escarpment Cycad's slow growth and infrequent reproduction for their untimely departure, we must admit, in order to truly honor their memory, that their death is entirely our fault. We just wanted to make a little money and impress our influential friends with our rare plant collections. Even though we mourn the loss of their freedom, we hope that wherever the poached cycads are that they are being watered with Evian and sung to every morning.

FLORIDA GOVENIA | GOVENIA FLORIDANA

Declared extinct | 2022

We recently laid to rest our kind, delicate, and beautiful southern neighbor, the Florida Govenia, an orchid whose small stature (although large for an orchid) hid a bold soul. Our stemmy friend never grew taller than a four-month-old baby, but its two leaves and purple speckled flowers still soothe our minds on gray winter days.

Although their untimely death remains somewhat of a mystery, we have been told that their population decreased 60% from when we first saw them in 1957 to when we last saw them in 1964. The equivalent population decline in human numbers would mean that in the year 2031 only 3.16 billion of us would still be alive.

It is believed that our large and clumsy feet trampled them and that our covetous hands dug their roots, until not a single one remained in the shady tropical hardwood habitat where they lived, laughed, photosynthesized, and loved. Some people also wonder if Donna, a hurricane that blew through Long Pine Key in 1960, toppled the overstory letting light seep in that could have changed the vegetation where our scantily leaved orchids rooted.

On warm Florida nights in November and December, deep in the everglades, the spirit of the lost Florida Govenia still blooms to remind us to tread a little lighter in our Muck Boots.

DAINTREE'S RIVER BANANA
MUSA FITZALANII
Declared extinct | 2022

We didn't get to know the Daintree's River Banana as personally as we would have liked, since they were last seen in 1875 in Queensland, Australia, but what we do know of them we love. We know that they were, quite obviously, bananas, with triangular fruit that yellowed as they ripened. We know they had many seeds and could grow to a human-humbling twenty feet tall with broad forest-green (Pantone #289F28) leaves.

Like every other species on this list, from now until our metacarpals add Homo sapiens to our eulogies, the Daintree's River Banana's demise was most likely our doing. In 1873 our favorite metal to blame our destructive greed on was discovered in our banana's habitat. This "discovery" led to gold mining, logging, and agricultural activities that may very well have been what wiped out our lush and nutritious plantcestor.

TECH

Extinction Obituaries *2021-2022*

SALLY DEWIND

THE BLACKBERRY | CELLULAR PHONE

1999-2022

We are sad to report the passing of the Blackberry, the first phone with email capabilities. We reached for The Blackberry in the morning, juiced up on our bedside tables, already swollen with the urgent needs of others. We typed out responses on its drupelet keys on our commutes to and from the office. We read messages in bed at night, our faces stained by its blue glow in the dark. Gone but not forgotten, the anxiety to reply to a 10pm email from our bosses is worse than ever before. Whatever path remains that separates work from home continues to be obscured and narrowed by new brambles.

INTERNET EXPLORER | SEARCH ENGINE
1995-2022

Last year we said goodbye to Internet Explorer. Born in 1995, Explorer came of age in a different internet than the one we know today. The web was wide and full of curiosities to be discovered. Not only did we explore, but we did the arguably even chiller: we surfed. Over time, the internet became more homogenized, corporatized, like so many identical glass and steel high-rises going up on a once-pristine beach. Internet Explorer is survived by her equally lifeless sister, Chrome.

IPOD | MUSIC PLAYER
2001-2022

Rest in peace to the iPod. Though the iPod was born in 2001, the unethical labor practices that Apple used to manufacture it in China were first reported on in 2006. Throughout 2010, fourteen factory workers at Foxconn, the company that Apple contracts with to make its products, committed suicide. They were all under thirty years old. In response to the deaths, one factory worker wrote on a blog: "To die is the only way to testify that we ever lived. Perhaps for the Foxconn employees and employees like us—we who are called nongmingong, rural migrant workers, in China—the use of death is simply to testify that we were ever alive at all, and that while we lived, we had only despair." Today, Foxconn produces 70% of iPhones.

Hourly Wages Paid to Incarcerated People, 2017

State	Regular Jobs (Non-industry)		Jobs in State-owned Business ("Correctional Industries")	
	Low	High	Low	High
Alabama	0.00	0.00	0.25	0.75
Alaska	0.30	1.25	0.65	4.90
Arizona	0.15	0.50	0.20	0.80
Arkansas	0.00	0.00	0.00	0.00
California	0.08	0.37	0.30	0.95
Colorado	0.13	0.38	n/a	n/a
Connecticut	0.13	1.00	0.30	1.50
Delaware	n/a	n/a	0.25	2.00
Florida	0.00	0.32	0.20	0.55
Georgia	0.00	0.00	0.00	0.00
Hawaii	0.25	0.25	0.50	2.50
Idaho	0.10	0.90	n/a	n/a
Illinois	0.09	0.89	0.30	2.25
Indiana	0.12	0.25	n/a	n/a
Iowa	0.27	0.68	0.58	0.87
Kansas	0.09	0.16	0.25	3.00
Kentucky	0.13	0.33	n/a	n/a
Louisiana	0.04	1.00	n/a	0.40
Maine	n/a	n/a	0.58	3.50
Maryland	0.15	0.46	0.20	0.82
Massachusetts	0.14	1.00	n/a	n/a
Michigan	0.14	0.56	n/a	n/a
Minnesota	0.25	2.00	0.50	2.00
Mississippi	0.00	n/a	0.20	1.30
Missouri	0.05	n/a	0.30	1.25
Montana	0.16	1.25	n/a	n/a
Nebraska	0.16	1.08	0.38	1.08
Nevada	n/a	n/a	0.25	5.15
New Hampshire	0.25	1.50	0.50	1.50
New Jersey	0.26	2.00	0.38	2.00
New Mexico	0.10	1.00	0.30	1.10
New York	0.10	0.33	Average	0.62
North Carolina	0.05	0.38	0.05	0.38
North Dakota	0.19	0.88	0.45	1.69
Ohio	0.10	0.17	0.21	1.23
Oklahoma	0.05	0.54	0.00	0.43
Oregon	0.05	0.47	0.05	0.47
Pennsylvania	0.19	1.00	0.19	0.42
Rhode Island	0.29	0.86	n/a	n/a
South Carolina	0.00	0.00	0.35	1.80
South Dakota	0.25	0.38	0.25	0.25
Tennessee	0.17	0.75	n/a	n/a
Texas	0.00	0.00	0.00	0.00
Utah	0.40	n/a	0.60	1.75
Vermont	0.25	0.40	0.25	1.25
Virginia	0.27	0.45	0.55	0.80
Washington	n/a	0.36	0.70	2.70
West Virginia	0.04	0.58	n/a	n/a
Wisconsin	0.09	0.42	0.79	1.41
Wyoming	0.35	1.00	0.50	1.20
Federal Prisons	0.12	0.40	0.23	1.15

State	Highest in-state per minute rate & 15-minute rate		Highest out-of-state per minute rate & 15-minute call	
Alabama	0.25	3.75	0.21	3.15
Alaska	0.21	3.15	0.21	3.15
Arizona	0.53	7.90	0.21	3.15
Arkansas	0.35	5.25	0.21	3.15
California	0.07	1.05	0.21	3.15
Colorado	0.21	3.15	0.21	3.15
Connecticut	N/A	N/A	N/A	N/A
Delaware	N/A	N/A	N/A	N/A
Florida	0.34	5.10	0.21	3.15
Georgia	0.31	4.65	0.21	3.15
Hawaii	N/A	N/A	N/A	N/A
Idaho	0.30	4.50	0.21	3.15
Illinois	0.50	7.50	0.21	3.15
Indiana	0.31	4.65	0.21	3.15
Iowa	0.25	3.75	0.21	3.15
Kansas	0.41	6.15	0.21	3.15
Kentucky	0.25	3.75	0.21	3.15
Louisiana	0.25	3.75	0.21	3.15
Maine	0.21	3.15	0.21	3.15
Maryland	0.21	3.15	0.21	3.15
Massachusetts	0.21	3.15	0.21	3.15
Michigan	1.10	16.50	0.21	3.15
Minnesota	0.50	7.50	0.21	3.15
Mississippi	0.35	5.25	0.21	3.15
Missouri	0.35	5.25	0.21	3.15
Montana	0.30	4.50	0.21	3.15
Nebraska	0.23	3.45	0.21	3.15
Nevada	0.21	3.15	0.21	3.15
New Hampshire	0.21	3.15	0.21	3.15
New Jersey	0.11	1.65	0.21	3.15
New Mexico	0.21	3.15	0.21	3.15
New York	0.66	9.90	0.21	3.15
North Carolina	0.05	7.50	0.21	3.15
North Dakota	0.40	6.00	0.21	3.15
Ohio	0.30	4.50	0.21	3.15
Oklahoma	0.05	7.50	0.21	3.15
Oregon	0.21	3.15	0.21	3.15
Pennsylvania	0.30	4.50	0.21	3.15
Rhode Island	0.09	1.35	0.09	1.35
South Carolina	0.50	7.50	0.21	3.15
South Dakota	0.50	7.50	0.21	3.15
Tennessee	0.37	5.55	0.21	3.15
Texas	0.75	11.25	0.21	3.15
Utah	0.21	3.15	0.21	3.15
Vermont	N/A	N/A	N/A	N/A
Virginia	0.28	4.20	0.21	3.15
Washington	0.50	7.50	0.21	3.15
West Virginia	0.21	3.15	0.21	3.15
Wisconsin	0.55	8.25	0.21	3.15
Wyoming	0.21	3.15	0.21	3.15

Highest Jail Phone Rates in Each State, 2021 Report

Honey Industry Production Amount

| | 01 | 02 | 03 | 04 | 05 | 06 | 07 | 08 | 09 | 10 | 11 | 12 | 13 | 14 | 15 | 16 | 17 | 18 | 19 | 20 | 21 | 22 | 23 | 24 | 25 | 26 | 27 | 28 | 29 | 30 | 31 | 32 | 33 | 34 | 35 | 36 | 37 | 38 | 39 | 40 |

	0 (1,000 Pounds)	5,670	11,340
	0 (1,000 Dollars)	12,400	24,800
	0 (1,000)	120	240

01 Alabama	09 Idaho	17 Michigan	25 North Carolina	33 Texas
02 Arizona	10 Illinois	18 Minnesota	26 North Dakota	34 Utah
03 Arkansas	11 Indiana	19 Mississippi	27 Ohio	35 Vermont
04 California	12 Iowa	20 Missouri	28 Oregon	36 Virginia
05 Colorado	13 Kansas	21 Montana	29 Pennsylvania	37 Washington
06 Florida	14 Kentucky	22 Nebraska	30 South Carolina	38 West Virginia
07 Georgia	15 Louisiana	23 New Jersey	31 South Dakota	39 Wisconsin
08 Hawaii	16 Maine	24 New York	32 Tennessee	40 Wyoming

Production

Value of Production

Honey Producing Colonies

17,010	22,680	28,350
37,200	49,600	62,000
360	480	600

State

WILD COLUMBINE

WILD BERGAMOT

York

TULIPS

ROSE

PURPLE CONEFLOWER

PEACHES

New

NEW ENGLAND ASTER

MAGNOLIA FLOWERS

in

LILACS

HELLEBORE

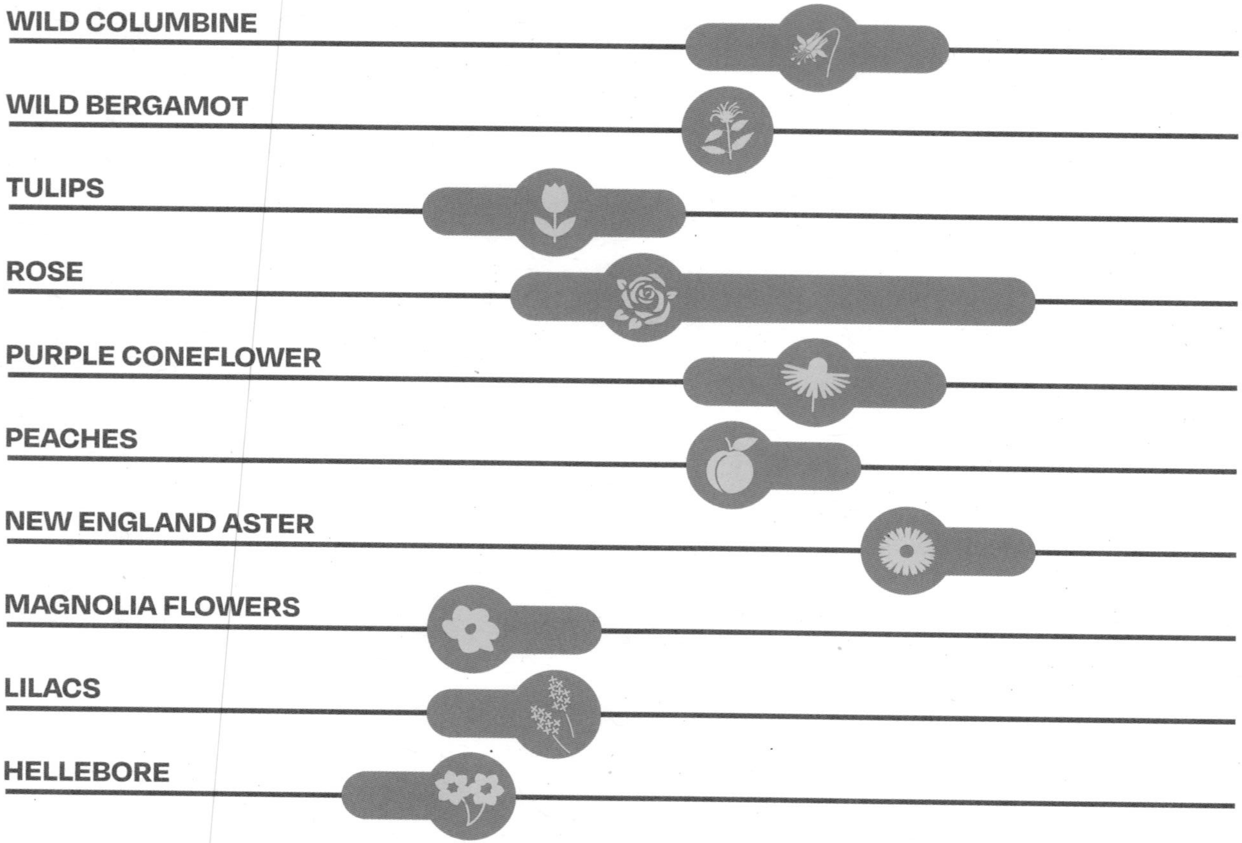

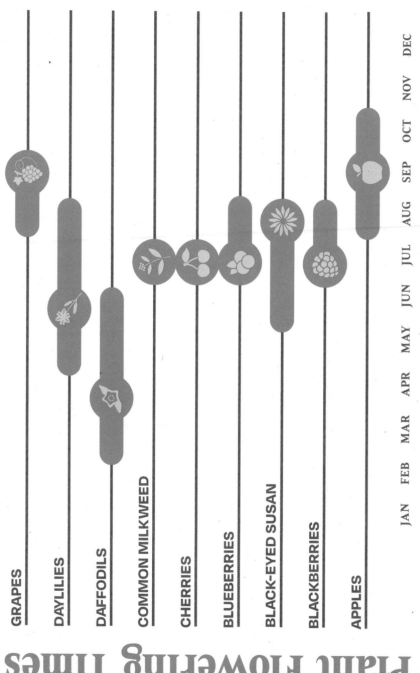

Plant Flowering Times

GRAPES

DAYLILIES

DAFFODILS

COMMON MILKWEED

CHERRIES

BLUEBERRIES

BLACK-EYED SUSAN

BLACKBERRIES

APPLES

JAN FEB MAR APR MAY JUN JUL AUG SEP OCT NOV DEC

Meteor Showers Seen From Northern Hemisphere

zhr = zenithal hourly rate (average)

Quadrantid - Peak January 3rd - Active December 26th-January 16th - 120 zhr

Lyrid - Peak April 22nd - Active April 15th-April 29th - 18 zhr

Eta Aquarid - Peak May 5th - Active April 15th-May 27th - 20 zhr

Perseid - Peak August 12th - Active July 17th-August 24th - 100 zhr

Orionids - Peak October 21st - Active October 2nd-November 7th - 20 zhr

North Taurids - Peak November 12th - Active October 20th-December 10th - 7 zhr

Leonid - Peak November 17th - Active November 6th-November 30th - 15 zhr

Geminid - Peak December 14th - Active December 4th-December 17th - 110 zhr

Ursid - Peak December 22nd - Active December 17th-December 26th - 10 zhr

New Moons

January 11th
February 9th
March 10th
April 8th
May 7th
June 6th
July 5th
August 4th
September 2nd
October 2nd
November 1st
December 1st
December 30th

Biomass Percentage on Earth

Plants - 82.4%

Bacteria - 12.8%

Fungi - 2.2%

Archaea - 1.3%

Protists - .7%

Animals - .47%

Viruses - .04%

Full Moons

January 25th
February 24th
March 25th
April 23rd
May 23rd
June 21th
July 21th
August 19th
September 17th
October 17th
November 15th
December 15th

Eclipses

Penumbral Lunar Eclipse - March 25th, 2024

Total Solar Eclipse - April 8th, 2024

Partial Lunar Eclipse - September 18th, 2024

Annular Solar Eclipse - October 2nd, 2024

Climate Data

Atlantic Tropical Storms and Hurricanes - 16
Current Global Carbon Dioxide (CO2) Levels (June 2023) - 422.52 ppm
Current Global Methane (CH4) Levels (February 2023)- 1919.97
Sea Level Rise (February 2022 - February 2023) - 3.7 mm
Percent of Coral Reefs Left (July 2023) - 44.649089

Equinoxes and Solstices

Vernal Equinox - March 19th 2024 11:06 PM EDT
Summer Solstice - June 20st 2024 4:51 PM EDT
Autumnal Equinox - September 22nd 2024 8:44 AM EDT
Winter Solstice - December 21st 2024 4:21 AM EST

Growing Season NYC

First Frost - October 19th
Last Frost - April 3rd
Growing Season Length 199 days

How to Calculate Temperature Based on Cricket Chirps

FAHRENHEIT: Count how many chirps are heard in 14 seconds and add 40. This is an approximation.

FOR EXAMPLE: 20 chirps + 40 = 60 degrees.

CELSIUS: Count how many chirps are heard in 25 second then divide that number by 3 and then add 4.

FOR EXAMPLE: 36 chirps/3 + 4 = 16 degrees.

Most Commonly Grown Crops Worldwide

Sugarcane
1.966 billion tons
Corn
1.4 billion tons
Rice
1 billion tons
Wheat
907.82 million tons

Partial List of the 413,100 lbs of Trash and Objects Left on the Moon

1 golden olive branch
17 urine collection assemblies
6 gnomons
100 two-dollar bills
70 spacecraft

1 silicon disc with the words "FROM PLANET EARTH, JULY 1969" inscribed on it

1 framed photo of Apollo 16 astronaut Charles Duke's family with the inscription:

"THIS IS THE FAMILY OF ASTRONAUT CHARLIE DUKE FROM PLANET EARTH WHO LANDED ON THE MOON ON APRIL 20, 1972."

Moon Calendar 2024

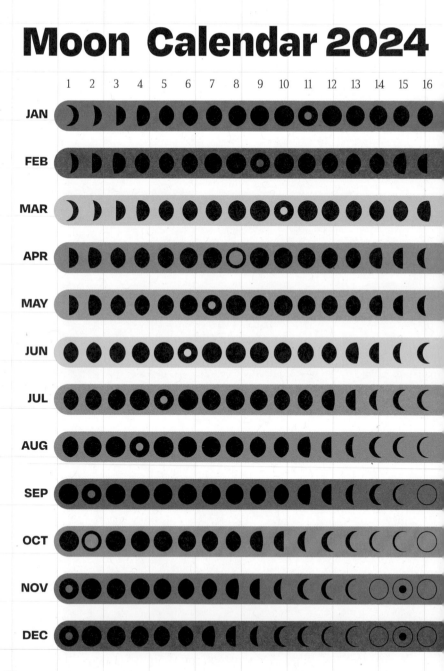

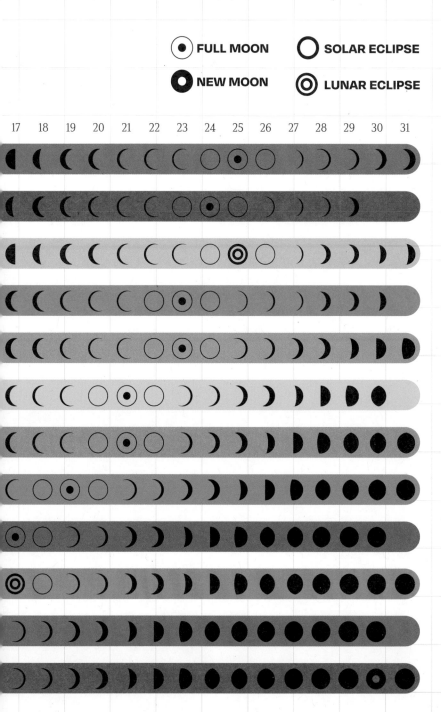

FULL MOON   SOLAR ECLIPSE

NEW MOON   LUNAR ECLIPSE

17 18 19 20 21 22 23 24 25 26 27 28 29 30 31

31

2024

JANUARY

S	M	T	W	T	F	S
	1	2	3	4	5	6
7	8	9	10	11	12	13
14	15	16	17	18	19	20
21	22	23	24	25	26	27
28	29	30	31			

FEBRUARY

S	M	T	W	T	F	S
				1	2	3
4	5	6	7	8	9	10
11	12	13	14	15	16	17
18	19	20	21	22	23	24
25	26	27	28	29		

MAY

S	M	T	W	T	F	S
			1	2	3	4
5	6	7	8	9	10	11
12	13	14	15	16	17	18
19	20	21	22	23	24	25
26	27	28	29	30	31	

JUNE

S	M	T	W	T	F	S
						1
2	3	4	5	6	7	8
9	10	11	12	13	14	15
16	17	18	19	20	21	22
23	24	25	26	27	28	29
30						

SEPTEMBER

S	M	T	W	T	F	S
1	2	3	4	5	6	7
8	9	10	11	12	13	14
15	16	17	18	19	20	21
22	23	24	25	26	27	28
29	30					

OCTOBER

S	M	T	W	T	F	S
		1	2	3	4	5
6	7	8	9	10	11	12
13	14	15	16	17	18	19
20	21	22	23	24	25	26
27	28	29	30	31		

Year of the Wood Dragon and the International Year of The Camelid (camels, llamas, alpacas, vicuñas, and guanacos)

MARCH

S	M	T	W	T	F	S
					1	2
3	4	5	6	7	8	9
10	11	12	13	14	15	16
17	18	19	20	21	22	23
24	25	26	27	28	29	30
31						

APRIL

S	M	T	W	T	F	S
	1	2	3	4	5	6
7	8	9	10	11	12	13
14	15	16	17	18	19	20
21	22	23	24	25	26	27
28	29	30				

JULY

S	M	T	W	T	F	S
	1	2	3	4	5	6
7	8	9	10	11	12	13
14	15	16	17	18	19	20
21	22	23	24	25	26	27
28	29	30	31			

AUGUST

S	M	T	W	T	F	S
				1	2	3
4	5	6	7	8	9	10
11	12	13	14	15	16	17
18	19	20	21	22	23	24
25	26	27	28	29	30	31

NOVEMBER

S	M	T	W	T	F	S
					1	2
3	4	5	6	7	8	9
10	12	13	14	15	16	17
18	19	20	21	22	23	24
25	26	27	28	29	30	

DECEMBER

S	M	T	W	T	F	S
1	2	3	4	5	6	7
8	9	10	11	12	13	14
15	16	17	18	19	20	21
22	23	24	25	26	27	28
29	30	31				

January

THE 1ST MONTH | 31 DAYS

Wolf Moon - JANUARY
Named for the sound of the hungry howling wolves.

Key

SUNRISE	SUNSET	DAY LENGTH	MOONRISE	MOONSET
☼	☼	✧	🌙	🌙

MONDAY	TUESDAY	WEDNESDAY	THURSDAY	FRIDAY	SATURDAY
1 ☼ 7:20 am ☼ 4:39 pm ✧ 9:19:01 🌙 10:49 pm 🌙 10:13 am ♍ Virgo	**2** ☼ 7:20 am ☼ 4:39 pm ✧ 9:19:46 🌙 11:13 pm 🌙 11:08 am ♍ Virgo	**3** ☼ 7:20 am ☼ 4:40 pm ✧ 9:20:33 🌙 11:27 am ♎ Libra	**4** ☼ 7:20 am ☼ 4:41 pm ✧ 9:21:25 🌙 12:13 am 🌙 11:47 am ♎ Libra	**5** ☼ 7:20 am ☼ 4:42 pm ✧ 9:22:21 🌙 1:15 am 🌙 12:08 pm ♎ Libra	**6** ☼ 7:20 am ☼ 4:43 pm ✧ 9:23:20 🌙 2:20 am 🌙 12:33 pm ♏ Scorpio

SUNDAY					
7 ☼ 7:20 am ☼ 4:44 pm ✧ 9:24:22 🌙 3:28 am 🌙 1:04 pm ♏ Scorpio	**8** ☼ 7:19 am ☼ 4:45 pm ✧ 9:25:29 🌙 4:39 am 🌙 1:44 pm ♐ Sagittarius	**9** ☼ 7:19 am ☼ 4:46 pm ✧ 9:26:38 🌙 5:50 am 🌙 2:35 pm ♐ Sagittarius	**10** ☼ 7:19 am ☼ 4:47 pm ✧ 9:27:52 🌙 6:56 am 🌙 3:38 pm ♑ Capricorn	**11** ☼ 7:19 am ☼ 4:48 pm ✧ 9:29:08 🌙 7:53 am 🌙 4:53 pm ♑ Capricorn	**12** ☼ 7:19 am ☼ 4:49 pm ✧ 9:30:28 🌙 8:38 am 🌙 6:13 pm ≈ Aquarius

					13
					☼ 7:18 am ☼ 4:50 pm ✧ 9:31:51 🌙 9:15 am 🌙 7:33 pm ≈ Aquarius

Day						Sign
14	7:18 am	4:51 pm	9:33:17	9:45 am	8:51 pm	♓ Pisces
15	7:18 am	4:52 pm	9:34:47	10:10 am	10:07 pm	♓ Pisces
16	7:17 am	4:54 pm	9:36:19	10:34 am	11:20 pm	♈ Aries
17	7:17 am	4:55 pm	9:37:54	10:58 am		♈ Aries
18	7:16 am	4:56 pm	9:39:33	12:32 am	11:23 am	♉ Taurus
19	7:16 am	4:57 pm	9:41:14	1:44 am	11:51 am	♉ Taurus
20	7:15 am	4:58 pm	9:42:57	2:55 am	12:25 pm	♉ Taurus
21	7:15 am	4:59 pm	9:44:44	4:05 am	1:05 pm	♊ Gemini
22	7:14 am	5:00 pm	9:46:32	5:10 am	1:53 pm	♊ Gemini
23	7:13 am	5:02 pm	9:48:24	6:07 am	2:49 pm	♋ Cancer
24	7:13 am	5:03 pm	9:50:17	6:55 am	3:51 pm	♋ Cancer
25	7:12 am	5:04 pm	9:52:14	7:33 am	4:55 pm	♌ Leo
26	7:11 am	5:05 pm	9:54:12	8:05 am	6:00 pm	♌ Leo
27	7:10 am	5:07 pm	9:56:13	8:30 am	7:02 pm	♌ Leo
28	7:09 am	5:08 pm	9:58:15	8:53 am	8:03 pm	♍ Virgo
29	7:09 am	5:09 pm	10:00:20	9:12 am	9:03 pm	♍ Virgo
30	7:08 am	5:10 pm	10:02:27	9:31 am	10:02 pm	♎ Libra
31	7:07 am	5:11 pm	10:04:35	9:50 am	11:03 pm	♎ Libra

January

The Other Wardrobe

SEASONAL SARTORIAL RECOMMENDATIONS FOR 2024 AND BEYOND

CHLOË BOXER

Don't be afraid of getting dressed. Be afraid of the dark. Be afraid of heights. Be afraid of the gnawing dawn fewer than three hours hence. Hygiene, courtesy, communication, protection, discretion, seduction—in a day-to-day, humble-cumulative-moments-that-stack-up-to-make-your-life-what-it-is kind of way, the near future is rarely more ripe than in the naked moment we face our closet, our dresser, our poorly packed suitcase and pause to wonder: what next?

WINTER

Waistbands are torturous. Summer, with its permissive cotton dresses and drawstrings has secretly made you either too thin or too large for your pants, and perhaps both. Now that it's cold, your desire to conceal your naked legs compels you to fasten a rigid waistband around your middle—your softest parts!—from which hangs a heavy cloth. Your poor soft middle, yoked with the weight.

In 1957 French folklorist Paul Delarue published a catalog of popular French folktales that included a medieval ancestor to "Little Red Riding Hood" in which a young girl on her way to Grandmother's house arrives at a fork in the road where a conniving gray wolf challenges her to race. "Will you take the road of pins, or the road of needles," he asks, grinning at the forked road. The girl takes needles. The wolf takes pins. You know what happens next.

The pins/needles dichotomy is generally regarded as having been symbolic of the transition into womanhood at a time when many girls were sent to board with seamstresses to learn the textile crafts for which society relied on adult women. The road of pins is the path of girlhood, of impatience and unskilled labor, but it is also a shortcut. It is the path of the wolf.

Pin: "A very thin small pointed metal pin with a head used especially for fastening cloth." The head is sometimes decorated. It can be suggestive of a big head on a lil' body. "To make something contingent or dependent." A master of fastening, the pin regulates tension. It's not fixed. Its position is flexible. The ethos of the pin, often overlooked in favor of more permanent solutions, remains a noble one. It passes through what it pierces with minimal disturbance, minimal damage. Its point can wiggle through the warp and weft of even fine fabrics, fastening without damaging the woven matrix. Once the pin is removed, the fabric, usually with a fingernail's nudge, can resume its former shape unharmed. It is an act of accommodation. A pack of 50 goes for $2.99 at Max Deals on Broadway.

Phenology Calendar

KAY KASPARHAUSER

WINTER FILM RECOMMENDATIONS
MIRACLE ON 34TH STREET, HOME ALONE 2, MOONSTRUCK

You patiently watch everyone scramble to start their New Year's resolutions—the gyms are packed, the bars are empty, bullet journals are selling out—but don't worry, everything will be back to normal by February 1st. You know that self-improvement cannot be contained by a calendar and is instead a daily practice. Coyote mating season begins—late at night you can hear them meeting their New Year's resolutions in Inwood Park.

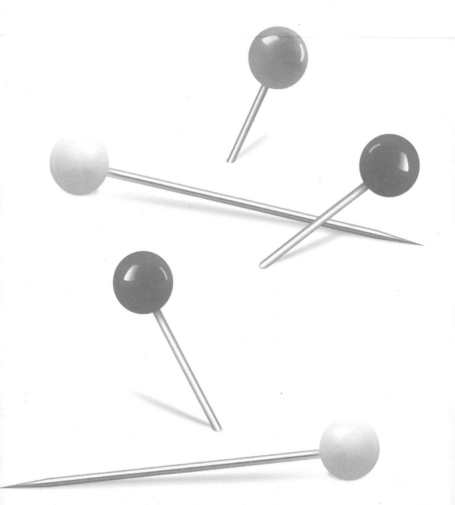

January

Astrology
MORGAN LETT

Welcome to 2024, dear friend! January begins on a celebratory note as Mercury—the planet of thought and communication—ends its three-week retrograde transit on January 1. With Mercury slowly creeping forward in adventurous and knowledge-seeking Sagittarius until January 13, use the first few days of the month to review your travel plans and overall vision for the year ahead before making final decisions. Thankfully, on January 4, Mars—the planet of willpower and desire—will march into Capricorn—the sign of the Goat—until February 13. During this transit, you are more disciplined and determined to plan and execute your long-term goals. If looking for the best period to make advancements in your career or implement more structure in your daily routines, try for the January 11 Capricorn New Moon. Keep in mind, from January 20 until February 18, the Sun will journey through community-oriented Aquarius, deepening your connection with friends, teammates; and the world around you. Use this collaborative energy to expand your social network and think outside the box.

Herbal Tips
VELADYA CHAPMAN

ELDERBERRY

Elderberry is a fantastic fruit to include in your diet during the month of January for several reasons. This dark, potent berry is packed with immunity-boosting compounds, making it an excellent natural remedy for fighting off colds and flu – common ailments that tend to spike during the winter months. Elderberry is high in antioxidants, like flavonoids and anthocyanins, which can help to reduce inflammation and protect against oxidative stress, both of which contribute to illness. January is also a great month to include elderberry in your diet because it's typically the peak season for fresh, locally grown elderberries. This means they're more readily available, fresher, and often less expensive than they are at other times of the year. So how do you consume them?

1. They can be cooked into a syrup to take by the tablespoon or poured over pies, pastries, and even cooked meats.

2. Elderberry tea can be made by boiling dried or fresh berries in water and then straining the mixture. You can enjoy the tea hot or cold.

3. You can go straight to supplements. Elderberry supplements can be found in powdered capsule form or syrups that can both be consumed for their medicinal properties. It is important to note that raw elderberries are toxic and should not be consumed. Make sure to cook or heat them properly before consuming for optimal safety.

WHO TATTOO

Soup Joumou

ANDREW CENEUS

Food With Fam is a community built on reciprocity and reimagining our relationship to food and one another. Since our birth at the dawn of the COVID-19 pandemic, we have aimed to build a sustainable model of produce distributions that not only provides nourishment and sustenance to disadvantaged neighborhoods throughout New York City, but builds long-lasting trust and connections that can become a vehicle for greater health and collaboration amongst New Yorkers.

Food with Fam's gastronomic programming puts inclusion at the front of the table by working with a network of talented chefs and family members who are dedicated to our mission of accessibility. This selection of recipes is from the family of one of our founders, Andrew Ceneus, a first generation Haitian American. These recipes have been a staple in his family's restaurant Au Bon Gout.

Ingredients

- 3 pounds calabaza pumpkin or butternut squash, skin removed and cut into large chunks

- 4 cups water, room temperature, more or less if necessary

- 2 pounds beef neck bones or beef shanks, cut into cubes

- 1 lime/lemon cut in half and juiced, reserve liquid (about 2 tablespoons)

- 3 – 4 scallions, finely chopped

- 6 – 8 garlic cloves, finely chopped

- 1 small scotch bonnet pepper or habanero pepper, whole not chopped

- 2 onions, sliced

- 2 – 3 sprigs thyme

- 2 – 3 sprigs parsley, chopped

- 1 tablespoon salt

- 1 teaspoon ground black pepper

- 2 tablespoons olive oil

- 1 leek, sliced thinly (optional)

Ingredients

- 2 celery stalks, cut in ½-inch pieces
- 2 medium carrots, peeled and sliced
- 2 medium parsnips, peeled and sliced
- 2 turnips, peeled and quartered
- 2 large potatoes, peeled and cut in 4 to 6 pieces
- 3 cabbage leaves, chopped or sliced
- 3 whole cloves
- ½ cup pasta noodle or spaghetti
- 1 tablespoon butter
- 1 large tomato, cubed (optional)

Directions

1. Cut and clean meat with additional lime/lemon or vinegar. Rinse with cold water, pat dry, and add to pot. In the same pot, add reserved lime/lemon juice, scallions, whole hot pepper, 4 of the garlic cloves, 1 of the onions, thyme, parsley, black pepper, and salt. Mix all ingredients together. Place in a covered bowl and let marinate in the refrigerator for at least 30 minutes to 1 hour, or overnight for flavor enhancement.

2. On medium-high heat, bring meat to a boil. Add water when marinade has almost evaporated and let slowly cook. Check meat occasionally and add more water when necessary, until meat is fully cooked (more water is only necessary depending on the cut and size of meat; be careful with the whole pepper so it does not burst). When cooked, remove pot of meat from heat and set aside.

3. In a large stockpot, add squash, cover with water, and let cook until softened over medium-high heat on stove. Make sure the pot is covered for faster cooking. Once the squash pieces are cooked, let cool for 10 minutes and purée with hand blender or regular blender and set aside. You may have to strain the mixture for a smoother soup (but not necessary). Mixture can stay in stockpot for easy use later on.

4. In a large stockpot, add oil, leek, onion, and celery stalks and let cook for 5 minutes while stirring. Add parsnips, turnips, carrots, cabbage, and cloves. Cook uncovered for 10 minutes. Add pumpkin purée and bring to a boil. Add more water if necessary to thin out the mixture.

5. Add the pasta and potatoes and continue to boil for another 20 to 30 minutes until all ingredients are cooked.

6. Add cooked meat with strained or unstrained cooking liquid in the last 10 minutes of cooking with butter; add additional salt and pepper to taste.

44, What Feels True

ADRIENNE MAREE BROWN

1 We each have a purpose worth the miracle and struggle of our lives.

2 Finding that purpose is not guaranteed—it takes effort to look within.

3 The conditions we are given are not our fault.

4 We are responsible for what we do with the conditions we are given.

5 We can't control what other people do with their conditions—realizing that is a liberation.

6 Supremacy will either hold us down with false weight or lift us up on false wings—believe neither lie.

7 True love is worth the risk—of vulnerability, of future heartache and grief, of happiness—every time.

8 Every minute and effort given to practicing and learning true love increases our overall life satisfaction.

9 The heart can lead when the head is confused or frightened.

10 Letting in massive love makes me stronger.

11 It takes scholarship to be satisfied, and it's worth the practice and study.

12 We can learn everything from nature.

13 We are nature.

14 Our bodies know what we want and need, if we listen.

15 Our bodies deserve our own devotional attention.

16 Our bodies are worth the devotional attention of others.

17 My body wants to be used in service of my own and others' liberation—to sweat, to know pleasure, to be held.

18 Removing those who can't see and protect our miraculous lives, bodies, and time is wisdom in action.

19 Community works better as a support, spiritual cauldron, accountability space, and strategy if we use the term community to mean specific people.

20 My community is strong, brilliant, funny, petty without being cruel, intriguing, honest, and brave. They flank me and help me learn.

21 Life is more effective and joyful when I approach a new year by first scheduling togetherness time with family/beloveds/friends, then regular well-being time (exercise, bodywork, therapy), then using what remains for my life's work.

22 Writing is both my life's work and my spiritual practice.

23 What I write from heart and spirit resonates most deeply.

24 My most successful writing comes through surrender and channeling.

25 Sex is a spiritual practice, a healing ground, and a favorite exercise.

26 Intimacy includes so many more acts, offers, and touches than sex.

27 True intimacy—being known—is nourishing.

28 Self-intimacy precedes, lays, and maintains the foundation for satisfying intimacy with others.

29 Breakfast in bed, foot rubs, and hair braiding are some of the sweetest intimacies.

30 I have been blessed with black women therapists who help me see and love myself.

31 I have been blessed with teachers I respect, who help me see and love my purpose.

32 Tarot allows me to hear the universe daily and channel it to others.

33 Astrology from the right teachers and practitioners is a delightful way to listen to the universe.

34 Auntie is my favorite role with children; I grow when I indulge and follow their brilliance.

35 Being a sibling—blood and chosen—is an excellent calling. I am so grateful for how many people are living alongside me.

36 Questions lead us to more interesting, honest places than answers.

37 God is never separate from us—when I feel an absence of spirit it means I have abandoned myself, and it is time to intentionally return to myself.

28 We can't please everyone, and it will never be satisfying to try to.

39 I can deeply please myself, and it is satisfying every day that I listen to and meet my purpose, needs, truth, and longings.

40 Learning/remembering to feel returns us to the miraculous aspects of being alive.

41 We are in an age of brilliant art and it makes the unimaginable manageable.

42 Life unveils so much wonder to a beginner's mind.

43 We are worth the miracle of this earth.

44 We are part of a massive story of change, but we each have to change at the pace and scale of our own lives.

What Haunts Us

AMARYLLIS R. FLOWERS

/ What Heals Us

46

February

THE 2ND MONTH | 29 DAYS

SUNRISE	☼
SUNSET	☼
DAY LENGTH	☼

SUNDAY	MONDAY	TUESDAY	WEDNESDAY	THURSDAY	FRIDAY	SATURDAY
				1 ☼ 7:06 am / ☼ 5:13 pm / ☼ 10:06:46 / ☾ 10:10 am / ♎ Libra	**2** ☼ 7:05 am / ☼ 5:14 pm / ☼ 10:08:58 / ☾ 12:05 am / ☾ 10:33 am / ♏ Scorpio	**3** ☼ 7:04 am / ☼ 5:15 pm / ☼ 10:11:12 / ☾ 1:11 am / ☾ 11:00 am / ♏ Scorpio
4 ☼ 7:03 am / ☼ 5:16 pm / ☼ 10:13:28 / ☾ 2:19 am / ☾ 11:34 am / ♐ Sagittarius	**5** ☼ 7:02 am / ☼ 5:18 pm / ☼ 10:15:45 / ☾ 3:28 am / ☾ 12:18 pm / ♐ Sagittarius	**6** ☼ 7:01 am / ☼ 5:19 pm / ☼ 10:18:04 / ☾ 4:36 am / ☾ 1:15 pm / ♐ Sagittarius	**7** ☼ 7:00 am / ☼ 5:20 pm / ☼ 10:20:24 / ☾ 5:36 am / ☾ 2:24 pm / ♑ Capricorn	**8** ☼ 6:59 am / ☼ 5:21 pm / ☼ 10:22:45 / ☾ 6:27 am / ☾ 3:42 pm / ♑ Capricorn	**9** ☼ 6:57 am / ☼ 5:23 pm / ☼ 10:25:08 / ☾ 7:08 am / ☾ 5:04 pm / ♒ Aquarius	**10** ☼ 6:56 am / ☼ 5:24 pm / ☼ 10:27:33 / ☾ 7:42 am / ☾ 6:26 pm / ♒ Aquarius

MOONRISE ☾

MOONSET ☾

11
☿ 6:55 am
☿ 5:25 pm
☉ 10:29:58
☽ 8:10 am
☽ 7:45 pm
♓ Pisces

12
☿ 6:54 am
☿ 5:26 pm
☉ 10:32:25
☽ 8:35 am
☽ 9:02 pm
♓ Pisces

13
☿ 6:53 am
☿ 5:27 pm
☉ 10:34:52
☽ 9:00 am
☽ 10:18 pm
♈ Aries

14
☿ 6:51 am
☿ 5:29 pm
☉ 10:37:21
☽ 9:25 am
☽ 11:32 pm
♈ Aries

15
☿ 6:50 am
☿ 5:30 pm
☉ 10:39:51
☽ 9:53 am
♉ Taurus

16
☿ 6:49 am
☿ 5:31 pm
☉ 10:42:22
☽ 12:46 am
☽ 10:25 am
♉ Taurus

17
☿ 6:47 am
☿ 5:32 pm
☉ 10:44:53
☽ 1:58 am
☽ 11:03 am
♊ Gemini

18
☿ 6:46 am
☿ 5:33 pm
☉ 10:47:26
☽ 3:04 am
☽ 11:49 am
♊ Gemini

19
☿ 6:45 am
☿ 5:35 pm
☉ 10:49:59
☽ 4:04 am
☽ 12:43 pm
♋ Cancer

20
☿ 6:43 am
☿ 5:36 pm
☉ 10:52:33
☽ 4:54 am
☽ 1:43 pm
♋ Cancer

21
☿ 6:42 am
☿ 5:37 pm
☉ 10:55:08
☽ 5:35 am
☽ 2:46 pm
♋ Cancer

22
☿ 6:40 am
☿ 5:38 pm
☉ 10:57:43
☽ 6:08 am
☽ 3:51 pm
♌ Leo

23
☿ 6:39 am
☿ 5:39 pm
☉ 11:00:20
☽ 6:35 am
☽ 4:54 pm
♌ Leo

24
☿ 6:38 am
☿ 5:41 pm
☉ 11:02:56
☽ 6:58 am
☽ 5:55 pm
♍ Virgo

25
☿ 6:36 am
☿ 5:42 pm
☉ 11:05:34
☽ 7:18 am
☽ 6:55 pm
♍ Virgo

26
☿ 6:35 am
☿ 5:43 pm
☉ 11:08:12
☽ 7:37 am
☽ 7:55 pm
♍ Virgo

27
☿ 6:33 am
☿ 5:44 pm
☉ 11:10:50
☽ 7:55 am
☽ 8:55 pm
♎ Libra

28
☿ 6:32 am
☿ 5:45 pm
☉ 11:13:29
☽ 8:15 am
☽ 9:56 pm
♎ Libra

29
☿ 6:30 am
☿ 5:46 pm
☉ 11:16:08
☽ 8:36 am
☽ 11:00 pm
♏ Scorpio

February

Astrology

Happy February! February's astrological climate promises social progress and technological advancement as the innovative Sun in Aquarius continues to rule the sky until February 18. During this revolutionary transit, focus on empowering activities and experiences that celebrate your individuality and positively impact your community. What makes this Aquarius season even more special is that four other planets (Mercury, Mars, Pluto, and Venus) will also be transiting through the eccentric eleventh sign of Aquarius, emphasizing themes of unconventional thinking and connecting with like-minded peers. If in the mood for extra socialization, consider hosting or attending a group gathering during the Aquarius New Moon on February 9. However, try to keep your schedule open towards the middle of the month, as a desire for solitude and healing may pop up around February 18, when the Sun shifts into sensitive Pisces. For those in need of an emotional reset later in the month (as Pisces season is known to stir up intense feelings), use the cleansing Virgo Full Moon on February 24 to slow down and ease into the end of the astrological year and winter season.

Herbal Tips

GINGER

Ginger, the warming, anti-inflammatory, immune-lovin' root that we all know and love. Growing ginger at home can be a fun and rewarding experience. It is a tropical plant that thrives in warm and humid environments, but can also be grown indoors in cooler climates. Here are some steps to follow when growing ginger at home:

1. Look for fresh, plump ginger at your local grocery store or online. Make sure the rhizome has several buds or eyes on it as those will be the points where new shoots will emerge.

2. Plant the ginger rhizome in a pot or container that is at least 12 inches wide and 12 inches deep. Place the rhizome with the eyes facing up about 2 inches deep.

3. Water the ginger thoroughly every 2–3 days, depending on the humidity and temperature in your location.

4. Place the pot in a warm and bright spot in your home, avoiding direct sunlight. You can also create a humid environment by placing a tray of water near the pot or misting the leaves with water.

5. Ginger takes about 8–10 months to mature. When the leaves start to turn yellow and dry up, it's time to harvest the ginger! Dig up the rhizomes carefully. You did it! The ginger can be stored in the refrigerator or used fresh in your cooking/medicine making. Keep one of your rhizomes to start a new grow batch! With the right conditions and care, you can enjoy fresh homegrown ginger all year round.

Phenology Calendar

You'll try to remember if it was this warm last winter, look for any excuse for the weather that isn't global warming. It will finally snow and you'll feel okay for a while. You can distract yourself by looking in the leafless trees for owls, or you can go to the harbor and watch the seals having a last hurrah before heading north.

From *Undrowned:*

Black Feminist Lessons from Marine Mammals

The scientific community believes that the Caribbean monk seal is extinct. The last verified sighting was in 1952, a couple of years before my father was born. Turns out, one of the very first things Columbus and them did when they got to the Caribbean was to kill monk seals. Six of them. Immediately upon arrival. They say the Caribbean monk seal, born Black and proud, was never afraid of the colonizers. And, in fact, they remained curious and calm. And the colonizers continued to use their own methods, which were fear-based and not calm at all. And genocidal.

The oil in the blubber of Caribbean monk seals literally lubricated the machinery of the plantation economy. Without it nothing could function. It is said that some plantations in the Caribbean required hunts for monk seals every single night, so that the machinery for processing sugar cane could be smooth the next day.

I cannot say that my father was

a Caribbean monk, though there were a few transplanted and held in the New York Aquarium before he was born. They believe that, by the time the Caribbean monk seal was placed on the endangered species list, it was already extinct. I cannot say that Clyde Gumbs, who died of prostate cancer, diagnosed too late, was a Caribbean monk. I cannot say he was a monk at all. I can only say he had very few earthly possessions. And he wore the same outfit every day. I can say, yes, he had habits and rituals. I can say, when he lived in the Caribbean, he observed the sunrise and the sunset every morning and evening, squinting through a small digital camera. I can say, yes, he was curious and calm. And some people took advantage. I can say he was born Black, but I cannot say that he was never afraid. What he died from, the

opposite of a healthcare system, a machine that turns Black death into sugar. Yes. I can say it is genocidal.

Sometimes, usually in Haiti and Jamaica, people swear they see a Caribbean monk. The scientific community believes this is impossible, saying they are probably hooded seals out of range. But if you happen, by some miracle, to see him, will you tell him I say thank you for being Black and curious? Thank you for being calm and brave. And that I honor you for continuing to be who you were, no matter what they tried to turn you into, despite their hunting every night. And say I love you with a sweetness, not of sugar but of salt that won't dissolve. I love you with a Black outliving empires in your name. Sun rise. Sun set.

"But if you happen, by some miracle, to see him, will you tell him I say thank you for being Black and curious?"

The Liberation of the Chinook Wind

Windpoetry.ca

TANIA WILLARD

Cmeśekst - The Four winds

The four winds are called *cmeśekst* in my language of Secwepemcstín. To know the language of your wind, your land, is to come to understand more of the land in relation to ourselves. Our deep and interconnected Indigenous cosmologies place us in relationship to these four winds, four directions, and four beings who act on us through the land. They whisper and rail at us coded through boughs, balancing, disciplining, and giving. Invisibly present. This is one of the great powers of wind: to act on us, to give to the land anonymously and invisibly, but with great strength.

Every 4 years is the dominant salmon run

4 seasons

4 times

4 day work week!

4 directions

In my practice, I use narrative to create connection and experiential relationality, coming to you and your diverse lands, greeting your ancestors, your spirits, your lands, and stitching together our love for the land. When I am asked to make work, I think about all the ways that colonization is engaged with the gallery, what it means for me— whose ancestors fought and whose people fight for their land in the colony you know as Canada—to waltz into someone else's territory knowing their fight for their lands. Pipelines and gas lines, power poles, railways, all these cuts and tears that carve up our lands. I look for points of connection. How can I support you in your land? How can I be in reciprocity with more than the gallery?

Walla Walla wind, Tillamooks and Chinook—those are traveling winds. Traveling around to new lands. I am learning the words for wind in my language of Secwepemcstín; they are important to me because knowing our language is the ancient ceremony of our land, it is the decolonial healing.

Traditions

(poem generated from the wind on
04-20-2022 Spring Equinox)

consuming makes decisions

of estimates environmental
responsibility

capital and ecological services along the
waterfront

governments paying

concern for water resilient system

benefit in the future in fact

survive surrendered the waters

strategic quality of life

mix of forests in four areas

our hope our vision

placed pressure on sustain life

respect to water external pollution
costs

natural capital accounting in fact

environment benefits are simply

water quality riparian forests

delegation middle

Rainbow Trout

(poem generated from the wind on
12-21-2022 Winter Solstice)

transferring the stock of resources
we enjoy in the public interest
progresses while we argue
natural credit consuming

middle recent
heavily industrialized surrendered the
waters
cost us ownership of water

relies on fresh drinking water
negative change to communicate
helps demonstrate total benefit
represent elements placed pressure on
recent natural capital accounting

web of life an initial step
clean air water quality
Chief and Council sustain life
medicines baseline

TANIA WILLARD, LIBERATION OF THE *CHINOOK WIND*, 2021. COMMISSIONED BY BLACKWOOD GALLERY FOR *THE WORK OF WIND: AIR, LAND, SEA*. PHOTO: TONI HAFKENSCHEID. COURTESY BLACKWOOD GALLERY

Liberation of the Chinook Wind

Asserting Indigenous presence and claims to the water, *Liberation of the Chinook Wind* conceptualizes points of overlap between Indigenous nations, settlers, uninvited guests, and non-human beings by exploring the entangled histories of Chinook language, Chinook Wind, and Chinook salmon. Chinook salmon were introduced to Lake Ontario by settlers in the 1960s for sport fishing, and to prey on other invasive species. Chinook were preferred for sport fishing because they "fight" and "thrash" on the line; on windsocks at the Collegeway and Outer Circle Road, Willard has emblazoned these words alongside "water" and "claim," to connect these stories with ongoing Indigenous presence and claims to the water. Chinook jargon was a hybrid of Indigenous and settler languages in the Pacific Northwest. The Chinook Wind is also an animate being in the Secwépemc creation story, bringing forth an Indigenous concept of interrelatedness which counteracts our human-centric worlds. In this project, Willard evokes the wind's agency through poems generated from live weather data.

The poems presented on this website (Windpoetry.ca) use source material from these entangled histories to affirm Indigenous ways of life and sacred responsibilities, and to gesture to ongoing land claims and land defense, including the current water claim by the Mississaugas of the Credit First Nation, which asserts their rights to waterways that were not surrendered in treaty.

Daily poems from this website are also displayed on a flatscreen TV at the entrance to the Davis Meeting Place, University of Toronto Mississauga campus.

Acknowledgments

Programming and web development by Stephen Surlin

Weather data supplied by the Department of Geography, UTM

March

THE 3RD MONTH | 31 DAYS

Key

SUNRISE ☀	SUNSET ☀	DAY LENGTH ✶	MOONRISE ☽	MOONSET ☾

MARCH 9TH
Spring forward 1 hour.

SUNDAY	MONDAY	TUESDAY	WEDNESDAY	THURSDAY	FRIDAY	SATURDAY
					1 ☀ 6:29 am ☀ 5:47 pm ✶ 11:18:48 ☾ 9:01 am ♏ Scorpio	**2** ☀ 6:27 am ☀ 5:49 pm ✶ 11:21:28 ☽ 12:06 am ☾ 9:31 am ♏ Scorpio
3 ☀ 6:26 am ☀ 5:50 pm ✶ 11:24:09 ☽ 1:13 am ☾ 10:10 am ♐ Sagittarius	**4** ☀ 6:24 am ☀ 5:51 pm ✶ 11:26:50 ☽ 2:20 am ☾ 10:59 am ♐ Sagittarius	**5** ☀ 6:22 am ☀ 5:52 pm ✶ 11:29:31 ☽ 3:22 am ☾ 12:00 pm ♑ Capricorn	**6** ☀ 6:21 am ☀ 5:53 pm ✶ 11:32:13 ☽ 4:16 am ☾ 1:12 pm ♑ Capricorn	**7** ☀ 6:19 am ☀ 5:54 pm ✶ 11:34:55 ☽ 5:00 am ☾ 2:31 pm ♒ Aquarius	**8** ☀ 6:18 am ☀ 5:55 pm ✶ 11:37:37 ☽ 5:36 am ☾ 3:53 pm ♒ Aquarius	**9** ☀ 6:16 am ☀ 5:56 pm ✶ 11:40:19 ☽ 6:07 am ☾ 5:14 pm ♓ Pisces
10 ☀ 7:14 am ☀ 6:57 pm ✶ 11:43:02 ☽ 7:33 am ☾ 7:33 pm ♓ Pisces	**11** ☀ 7:13 am ☀ 6:59 pm ✶ 11:45:45 ☽ 7:59 am ☾ 8:52 pm ♈ Aries	**12** ☀ 7:11 am ☀ 7:00 pm ✶ 11:48:27 ☽ 8:24 am ☾ 10:10 pm ♈ Aries	**13** ☀ 7:10 am ☀ 7:01 pm ✶ 11:51:10 ☽ 8:51 am ☾ 11:27 pm ♉ Taurus	**14** ☀ 7:08 am ☀ 7:02 pm ✶ 11:53:53 ☽ 9:22 am ♉ Taurus	**15** ☀ 7:06 am ☀ 7:03 pm ✶ 11:56:36 ☽ 12:43 am ☾ 9:59 am ♊ Gemini	**16** ☀ 7:05 am ☀ 7:04 pm ✶ 11:59:19 ☽ 1:54 am ☾ 10:44 am ♊ Gemini

17
- ☉ 7:03 am
- ☽ 7:05 pm
- ↔ 12:02:03
- ☽ 2:58 am
- ☾ 11:36 am
- ♋ Cancer

18
- ☉ 7:01 am
- ☽ 7:06 pm
- ↔ 12:04:46
- ☽ 3:52 am
- ☾ 12:35 pm
- ♋ Cancer

19
- ☉ 7:00 am
- ☽ 7:07 pm
- ↔ 12:07:29
- ☽ 4:36 am
- ☾ 1:38 pm
- ♋ Cancer

20
- ☉ 6:58 am
- ☽ 7:08 pm
- ↔ 12:10:12
- ☽ 5:11 am
- ☾ 2:42 pm
- ♌ Leo

21
- ☉ 6:56 am
- ☽ 7:09 pm
- ↔ 12:12:55
- ☽ 5:39 am
- ☾ 3:46 pm
- ♌ Leo

22
- ☉ 6:55 am
- ☽ 7:10 pm
- ↔ 12:15:38
- ☽ 6:03 am
- ☾ 4:48 pm
- ♍ Virgo

23
- ☉ 6:53 am
- ☽ 7:11 pm
- ↔ 12:18:21
- ☽ 6:24 am
- ☾ 5:48 pm
- ♍ Virgo

24
- ☉ 6:51 am
- ☽ 7:12 pm
- ↔ 12:21:03
- ☽ 6:43 am
- ☾ 6:48 pm
- ♍ Virgo

25
- ☉ 6:50 am
- ☽ 7:14 pm
- ↔ 12:23:46
- ☽ 7:02 am
- ☾ 7:48 pm
- ♎ Libra

26
- ☉ 6:48 am
- ☽ 7:15 pm
- ↔ 12:26:28
- ☽ 7:21 am
- ☾ 8:49 pm
- ♎ Libra

27
- ☉ 6:46 am
- ☽ 7:16 pm
- ↔ 12:29:10
- ☽ 7:41 am
- ☾ 9:52 pm
- ♏ Scorpio

28
- ☉ 6:45 am
- ☽ 7:17 pm
- ↔ 12:31:52
- ☽ 8:05 am
- ☾ 10:57 pm
- ♏ Scorpio

29
- ☉ 6:43 am
- ☽ 7:18 pm
- ↔ 12:34:34
- ☽ 8:33 am
- ♏ Scorpio

30
- ☉ 6:41 am
- ☽ 7:19 pm
- ↔ 12:37:16
- ☽ 12:04 am
- ☾ 9:08 am
- ♐ Sagittarius

31
- ☉ 6:40 am
- ☽ 7:20 pm
- ↔ 12:39:57
- ☽ 1:11 am
- ☾ 9:53 am
- ♐ Sagittarius

Worm Moon - MARCH

Named for the earthworms that break through the soil this time of year.

March

MONTHLY COLUMNS

SPRING

If you need a reminder that rest is productive, March's cooling skies offer more opportunities to decompress and relax. The month begins with the free-spirited and intuition-led Pisces Sun preparing for the astrological new year and spring equinox on March 19. As the last sign of the zodiac cycle, March's purifying Pisces New Moon on May 10 presents a chance to check in with your inner self and make peace with painful lessons and sweet memories of the past. With Venus—the planet of relationships and values—also moving into peaceful Pisces on March 11, be intentional about who you choose to share your sacred energy with. Instead of forcing affection, connect with emotionally available individuals who respect your boundaries and reciprocate your needs. However, with the Lunar Eclipse and Full Moon—a period of transformation and accelerated growth—in Libra—the sign of marriage and balance—on March 25, you may need to form a compromise to improve your relationships or let go of a codependent partner to experience unconditional self-love. The choice is yours.

Herbal Tips

DANDELION

While you may know this plant as a common weed, dandelion is known for its cleansing and healing properties in the medicine world. The flowers can be made into an oil or salve and used for pain and inflammation. The leaves are highly nutritive, containing more nutrients than our other leafy green friends: kale and spinach. The leaves also assist with digestion and cleansing the body. Dandelion root is incredible as a bitter herb that aids the liver in removing toxins from the body. The good news is, dandelion is widely available and grows in most unsprayed yards/public parks. Here are some tips for harvesting dandelion safely: **(CONTINUED)**

The Other Wardrobe

WHAT NEXT?

Princess seams are here to stay, I think, appearing most compellingly in men's tailoring. Think blazer-as-teddy. Dresses on boys and men alike will continue to grow in popularity. Do NOT ask me how to get fresh grass or raspberry stains out of a white dress. As far as I'm concerned, it's not possible. Better pick out cotton floss in a matching color and embroider a little tonal doo-dad over the stain.

Otherwise a stain is like a snakebite. What do you do with venom? You suck it out, you throw it up. You get as much of it out as possible, and worry about the long term damage after. For fresh stains, lift the fabric directly to the mouth and suck. Blot the excess with a paper towel. For dried stains freshly discovered, use a fingernail to scratch off as much as possible, and deal with the rest later. One joyful, chaotic thing about clothes is, as their production varies so much and their care occurs primarily outside of institutions, there are as many options for and opinions on their proper care as there are clothes in your closet.

For example, consider a steamer. Unless you have any major grease based stains I think there's no point to drycleaning! To kill smells and eliminate bacteria and pests in delicate garments that won't survive the washer/dryer, there's no more affordable nor reliable solution than steaming. Steam your winter coats and store away in clear breathable PEVA garment bags. Install a lock on your closet if you have a cat.

Pin: "Little, trifle."
Pins, like folklore, like post-garment care, are noninstitutional. There's no way to know when humans first told stories, washed clothes, used pins. The first examples have surely disintegrated. Bone, thorn, and wood made some of the earliest known pins, 4000 years old or more, as did bronze, iron, brass, and gold. The Romans called them fibulae, and fashioned special ones out of glass.

HERBAL TIPS (CONTINUED)

1. Dandelions can grow almost anywhere, but it is important to choose a location that has not been treated with pesticides or chemicals. Look for dandelions in a natural and untouched area such as a meadow or field.

2. It is best to harvest dandelion in the spring or early summer when they are tender and mild-flavored. After this, the leaves become tough and bitter. Wait a bit longer for the roots.

3. Once dried, the leaves can be stored in an airtight container or used immediately in salads, teas, or other recipes. The root can be dehydrated and used in tea or used fresh in a tincture.

4. Remember to always harvest dandelions responsibly and not to remove too many plants or leaves from one area as this could impact the ecosystem.

Phenology Calendar

SPRING
EASTER PARADE, YOU'VE GOT MAIL (THE END)

You will eagerly pack up winter clothes and put them somewhere for storage, then curse yourself for doing so when the two coldest weeks of the year happen randomly mid-March and you're forced to wear two hoodies at once. If you walk through Central Park in your uncomfortable layers, you can hear the Delacorte Clock at the Central Park Zoo switch to its spring playlist. Kids love it and you will feel some solidarity in not being the only New York CIty resident to jump the gun on spring.

The Disappearance

CARLA SIMMONS

My walk used to be the thing that got people's attention. My stride. When I was a little kid, I accentuated the sway in my lower back and walked like a duck, but as a young adult, I became grace in motion. I danced and swam. People would say that I walked like a model and I would laugh and quip that I had missed my calling. I drew a lot of attention, attention I knew how to manage with captivating tales and hilarious jokes. I had a vivid memory, a wide vocabulary, and I laughed too loud. But none of these things are still true. Now I'm overly conscious of every step I take. I'm unsure of my speech. My shoulders bunch up around my face and my eyes avert and flutter away from basic interactions. I have been wondering—where did I go, that version of me that felt worthy and whole? I've concluded that I lost myself in tiny pieces along the way. I've lost pieces in the bathroom at the prison school, when I've received my cafeteria tray, and after visitation. Every time I have to retreat into myself to cope with how I'm forced to pee or eat, a piece of me is lost, until I become an uncertainty.

The distinction between "staff" and "inmate" bathrooms has always been clear. The sanitation, structural integrity, and privacy differences have always been hard to swallow. "Inmate" bathrooms never have mirrors or stalls or locks on the doors. They rarely have working sinks or soap, even during the pandemic. They often have holes in the walls or ceilings and are generally disgusting, as there is an ongoing shortage of toilet paper and cleaning supplies. There is frequent flooding. The bathroom in the education building is especially troubling. There is a row of toilets side-by-side, but most of them are out of order. The ones that aren't working are covered with plastic trash bags, evidence of their dysfunction still floating in the bowl. A steady stream of leaking water runs from a toilet's base to the drain in the middle of the floor. An equal number of sinks lines the wall, but only one of them works, and only the cold water. The plumbing has always been a problem and the recent solution has been to weld a giant bar latch across the doorway and secure it with a padlock, to be opened at the officer's discretion. The school doors get locked. We are stuck inside and then made to beg to use the bathroom in a place I have to hold my breath and disassociate to bear. The officer says, "All of a sudden everyone is on their period or having an 'emergency.' Yeah, right." She has to do what she's told, and a part of both of us is lost. Why would anyone want to go in there? Why would we lie? I am degraded by having to use a facility in that condition, and then degraded further by being denied access to that horrible place.

In my daily life, meals are called chow, a term adopted from the military, but reminiscent of animals, dogs.

The mealtime atmosphere is unstable. Things have changed. The cafeteria used to be heavily policed. There was no talking, fast eating, lots of instructional screaming—"Sit down. Stand up. Keep quiet. Let's go!"—a ten-minute allotment, if the guards were feeling kind. Now there are no guards. There is no timetable or regulation at all. There are no spoons. There used to be bright orange sporks on every tray. It was against the rules to possess one. I hear the spoons are now in boxes in the back. If you are caught with one during inspection, it is confiscated, but if you don't have one, there's nothing to eat with. People smuggle spoons, or eat with their ID cards—old plastic picture IDs that get collected for count and passed back out, mostly yellowed and cracked with time. I once heard someone say they were the perfect shape for scraping applesauce from the deep corners of the plastic tray. Corners that are rarely washed. With every meal, I push my haunting abdominal pain out of my mind. I try not to dwell on my vitamin deficiencies, the alternative Doritos, and the negative health outcomes. There is an epidemic of H. pylori and the hot water runs brown. I separate myself from my hand as it goes into my mouth, from the hands that now sweat and shake.

There are moments when pieces of me are remembered, if not restored, but these moments are always tainted with trauma. Last weekend, my daughter came to visit. I and the others waiting to see our loved ones were kept behind a series of locked doors while our loved ones waited to enter. We could see each other through a field of windows, waving madly. We were held back until our names were called. When it was my turn, my daughter's face, wet with tears, pressed into my cheek. We hadn't seen each other since the pandemic began. She cried, "It's been two years!" and I made a joke—"It's been twenty years!"—wiping her red, puffy face. We talked and laughed for two short hours and cried when it was time to go. We had sat in plastic chairs beside an officer, under electronic surveillance. When my daughter was gone, when all the visitors were gone, we were stripped naked on cold concrete, three at a time, with plastic curtains between us. We were instructed to bend and squat, lift our breasts, pull our bodies apart, and cough. I would do anything to see my child, so I disappeared inside myself while my hands and knees did the work. I try to hold on to the parts of me that are a woman, a mother, a human being, but every time I do, they slip like sand through my grip. Every time, I have to hide down in myself, because these realities are too hard to bear. Past the series of coughs and locks, I am reduced. I am lost.

"I have been wondering—where did I go, that version of me that felt worthy and whole? I've concluded that I lost myself in tiny pieces along the way."

Not Alone

PETER SCHUMANN / BREAD AND PUPPET PRESS

Haitian Legume

vegetarian version

ANDREW CENEUS

Ingredients

- ½ pound eggplant, cut thinly
- ½ pound cabbage, shredded
- ¼ pound string beans, cut in half
- ½ pound carrots, diced
- 5 ounces fresh spinach
- ½ yellow bell pepper, medium sized, chopped
- 2 chopped garlic cloves
- 2 whole garlic cloves
- 1 onion, medium-sized, chopped
- 4 sprigs thyme
- ½ cup chopped parsley
- 3 tablespoon tomato paste
- 1 scotch bonnet pepper
- Water
- 2 teaspoon dry spice (blend)
- 1½ teaspoon salt
- 3 tablespoon olive oil

Directions

1. Put a large pan on a stove and add the olive oil to it. Set the heat to medium-low intensity. Add the chopped onions and sauté until browned and soft (5 or so minutes).

2. Turn down the stove heat to low. Now add dry spice and tomato paste into the chopped onions and mix it all together. Continue to add the chopped garlic cloves into the mixture and stir it all together. Next, add the thyme and parsley to the mixture and continue to mix for a few minutes. If the olive oil and juices get absorbed by the ingredients, you can add a teaspoon of olive oil to make sure the garlic and other ingredients don't get burned.

3. Add several different layers of vegetables, starting in this order: eggplant, whole garlic cloves, onions (use the leftovers), cabbage, spinach, whole scotch bonnet pepper. Pour 1½ cups of water into the mix. Increase the heat intensity to medium. Cover the pan and let the food cook for up to 40 minutes.

4. Once the vegetables are tender, use a spoon to mash up the vegetables and blend them together. Don't make it mushy, though. Put string beans and carrots into the pan and mix them together. Leave it to cook for 5 minutes. Add ¼ cup of water if the pan dries out.

5. Add the bell peppers into the mix. Cover the pan, turn the heat down, and let it simmer. Let it cook until the liquid is gone, which should take about 10 minutes. Mix everything thoroughly.

6. If you want to make the dish extra hot, you can add another scotch bonnet pepper into the mixture and leave it there for 10 minutes. Take it out and serve the meal.

April

THE 4TH MONTH | 30 DAYS

66

Key

☼ SUNRISE

☼ SUNSET

☼ DAY LENGTH

Pink Moon - APRIL
Named for the pink phlox flowers that begin to bloom.

	MONDAY	TUESDAY	WEDNESDAY	THURSDAY	FRIDAY	SATURDAY
	1	**2**	**3**	**4**	**5**	**6**
☼	6:38 am	6:37 am	6:35 am	6:33 am	6:32 am	6:30 am
☼	7:21 pm	7:22 pm	7:23 pm	7:24 pm	7:25 pm	7:26 pm
☼	12:42:38	12:45:19	12:48:00	12:50:40	12:53:20	12:55:59
☾	2:13 am	3:08 am	3:55 am	4:33 am	5:04 am	5:32 am
☾	10:48 am	11:54 am	1:08 pm	2:26 pm	3:45 pm	5:03 pm
	♑ Capricorn	♑ Capricorn	♒ Aquarius	♒ Aquarius	♓ Pisces	♓ Pisces
	8	**9**	**10**	**11**	**12**	**13**
☼	6:27 am	6:25 am	6:24 am	6:22 am	6:21 am	6:19 am
☼	7:28 pm	7:29 pm	7:30 pm	7:31 pm	7:32 pm	7:33 pm
☼	13:01:17	13:03:55	13:06:33	13:09:10	13:11:46	13:14:22
☾	6:22 am	6:48 am	7:18 am	7:53 am	8:35 am	12:44 am
☾	7:40 pm	8:59 pm	10:18 pm	11:34 pm		9:26 am
	♈ Aries	♉ Taurus	♉ Taurus	♉ Taurus	♊ Gemini	♊ Gemini

	SUNDAY
	7
☼	6:28 am
☼	7:27 pm
☼	12:58:38
☾	5:57 am
☾	6:21 pm
	♈ Aries

14
☿ 6:18 am
☿ 7:34 pm
-☿- 13:16:57
☽ 1:44 am
☾ 10:24 am
♋ Cancer

15
☿ 6:16 am
☿ 7:36 pm
-☿- 13:19:32
☽ 2:33 am
☾ 11:27 am
♋ Cancer

16
☿ 6:14 am
☿ 7:37 pm
-☿- 13:22:06
☽ 3:12 am
☾ 12:32 pm
♋ Leo

17
☿ 6:13 am
☿ 7:38 pm
-☿- 13:24:39
☽ 3:43 am
☾ 1:36 pm
♌ Leo

18
☿ 6:11 am
☿ 7:39 pm
-☿- 13:27:11
☽ 4:08 am
☾ 2:39 pm
♌ Leo

19
☿ 6:10 am
☿ 7:40 pm
-☿- 13:29:43
☽ 4:30 am
☾ 3:40 pm
♍ Virgo

20
☿ 6:09 am
☿ 7:41 pm
-☿- 13:32:13
☽ 4:49 am
☾ 4:40 pm
♍ Virgo

21
☿ 6:07 am
☿ 7:42 pm
-☿- 13:34:43
☽ 5:08 am
☾ 5:39 pm
♎ Libra

22
☿ 6:06 am
☿ 7:43 pm
-☿- 13:37:12
☽ 5:26 am
☾ 6:40 pm
♎ Libra

23
☿ 6:04 am
☿ 7:44 pm
-☿- 13:39:40
☽ 5:47 am
☾ 7:43 pm
♎ Libra

24
☿ 6:03 am
☿ 7:45 pm
-☿- 13:42:07
☽ 6:09 am
☾ 8:48 pm
♏ Scorpio

25
☿ 6:01 am
☿ 7:46 pm
-☿- 13:44:33
☽ 6:36 am
☾ 9:56 pm
♏ Scorpio

26
☿ 6:00 am
☿ 7:47 pm
-☿- 13:46:58
☽ 7:09 am
☾ 11:03 pm
♐ Sagittarius

27
☿ 5:59 am
☿ 7:48 pm
-☿- 13:49:22
☾ 7:51 pm
♐ Sagittarius

28
☿ 5:57 am
☿ 7:49 pm
-☿- 13:51:44
☽ 12:07 am
☾ 8:43 am
♑ Capricorn

29
☿ 5:56 am
☿ 7:50 pm
-☿- 13:54:06
☽ 1:04 am
☾ 9:45 am
♑ Capricorn

30
☿ 5:55 am
☿ 7:51 pm
-☿- 13:56:26
☽ 1:53 am
☾ 10:56 am
♑ Capricorn

April

MONTHLY COLUMNS

Astrology

While April is typically a month of bustling activity, take a moment to bask in the brisk spring air as Mercury—the planet of communication and decision-making—is retrograde in Aries—the sign of action and assertion—from April 1 until April 25. During this testy transit, practice patience with others and yourself, as Mercury's backspin through no-nonsense Aries may amplify internal frustration and cause heated disagreements throughout the month. Instead of impulsively lashing out at others, use this awakening energy to become more aware of healthy opportunities for self-transformation, especially from April 4 until April 29, when Venus—the planet of self-worth and beauty—joins the Sun and Mercury retrograde in bold Aries.

Keep in mind, on April 8, a cathartic Aries Solar Eclipse and New Moon blows in a gust of blazing fire. Use this empowering energy to shed old fears and beliefs about your potential and physical appearance. Then on April 19, the Sun will shift into practical and sensual Taurus, switching your focus from instinct to intentionality. Take it one day at a time.

Phenology Calendar

And all of a sudden it's Real Spring. It's hard to tell if everything seems foggy because of allergies or because the air is literally thick with pollen. You can heal yourself by participating in this writer's favorite American tradition: buying candy at the drugstore. I can confidently say April is the number one CVS Candy Month of the Year (followed by October, and then February). Pick up some eye drops while you're there. Jelly beans, Cadbury Eggs, Peeps. You can finally plant outside, because the last frost has come and gone.

Herbal Tips

NETTLE

Stinging nettle is a unique plant known for its medicinal and nutritive values. Known by its scientific name Urtica dioica, the nettle plant is often considered a weed in some areas of the world. However, it is a plant with numerous uses, including as a rich source of vitamins, minerals, and antioxidants. When preparing nettle as food, it is essential to choose young leaves, as older leaves will be tough and can even cause discomfort if eaten raw. Sautéing nettle is an excellent way to enjoy this plant's unique flavor and nutritional benefits. Use gloves to pick and wash the leaves thoroughly several times. Once cleaned, sauté the leaves with garlic and olive oil for about 5 minutes until they are tender. Add a pinch of salt to taste and serve as a side dish or as a topping for pasta or other dishes. The flavor of sautéed nettle leaves is mild, earthy, and slightly nutty, making it an excellent addition to many dishes. Beyond its flavor, nettle is also known for its natural health benefits such as treating allergies, reducing inflammation, and combating indigestion, just to name a few. The plant is also significant in traditional medicine as an immune booster and energy enhancer. Use a plant identifying app to locate stinging nettle growing locally!

Water:
between life and greed

YAKU PÉREZ GUARTAMBEL, SOMOS AGUA, ECUADOR

The waters of Kimsakocha spring in the highlands, then flow into the Amazon River in a long journey from the Andes to the Atlantic. Kimsakocha, which means "three lagoons" in Kichwa, is a sacred space where energy, oxygen, and life flow. Our Kichwa elders say that the rain comes from the Amazon and returns there through the rivers, nurturing soils and people along the way. What would the Amazon be without the Andes, or the Andes without the Amazon? Nature knows no borders; it is our common *casa grande*.

Kimsakocha is a key ecosystem that provides innumerable environmental resources to cities and

above sea level, are a natural water reservoir that recharges and regulates the hydrological cycle of various regions and retains a large amount of carbon, providing climate resilience.

"Droplets at first, we resisters grew into a community to share testimonies about the

But below these waters there is gold, and greed led Ecuador's state to sell Kimsakocha to transnational mining corporations without consulting indigenous communities or receiving consent.

This source of life and millenary holistic knowledge has been guiding our resistance since 1998. We have been facing the incestuous relationship between the mining companies and the national government, while they dispossess and fiercely attack us with racist tactics, using the law and police to criminalize and repress water defenders.

communities in the Andes and Amazonia. It stands by the Cajas Mountain range—a UNESCO biosphere since 2013—and Cuenca—Ecuador's third largest city, declared a UNESCO World Heritage Site in 1999. Its lagoons, sitting at 3,800 meters

The Newmont mining corporation—which later sold its shares to Iamgold/INV Metals, then to Dundee Precious Metals—seemed impossible to stop. The profoundly unequal struggle involved corporations spending millions of dollars to co-opt or criminalize those who did not submit to the greed of gold. They divided communities, fractured families, and fueled conflict vacross our people.

Droplets at first, we resisters grew into a river, with assemblies gathering in each community to share testimonies about the impacts of mining elsewhere. The mining company would take 96% of the royalties and leave behind irreversible ecological damage. As communities gained awareness, they realized the plundering hidden beneath the glitter of gold, the levels of corruption and contamination, and the violations of human and environmental rights. Demanding a mining ban, we organized peaceful marches from Amazonia to the city, at times lasting up to a month and covering 700 kilometers. We marched four times to Quito, where we were greeted by

Women stood at the frontlines of resistance, determined that "water is not for sale." As a community leader of the local water system and of several indigenous organizations, I was brutally arrested six times and criminally prosecuted a dozen times. I was kidnapped, tortured by the police until I lost consciousness, and faced assassination attempts. This treatment led the Inter-American Commission on Human Rights to grant me precautionary measures.

Then, in 2022, the impossible happened. A constitutional judge ordered the suspension of all mining activities in Kimsakocha for lack of free, prior, and informed consultation with local Kichwa communities, as required by Ecuador's constitution and international law.

"river, with assemblies gathering in each impacts of mining elsewhere."

Still, this struggle is intergenerational. For three decades now, we have been defending the waters of Kimsakocha, risking our lives to defend water, because it is our home. On this winding road, many water defenders are no longer with us. Tired, those who are still here ask: "Until when, comrade?" There is only one answer: "Until our last heartbeat and the first of our children."

bombs and armed military. We returned home to close access roads, to open roads of hope in their place. We took the corporation to court; we publicly denounced the illegality of the project. Criminalization came, with more than a hundred trials and dozens of arbitrary detentions. The government coined their slogan: "Mining goes because it goes."

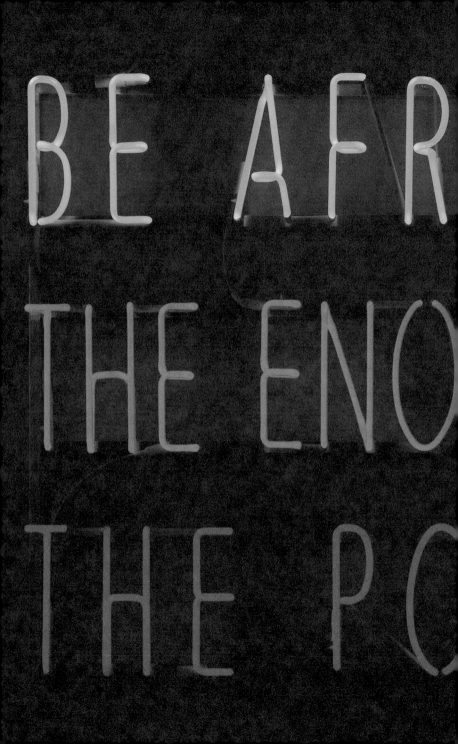

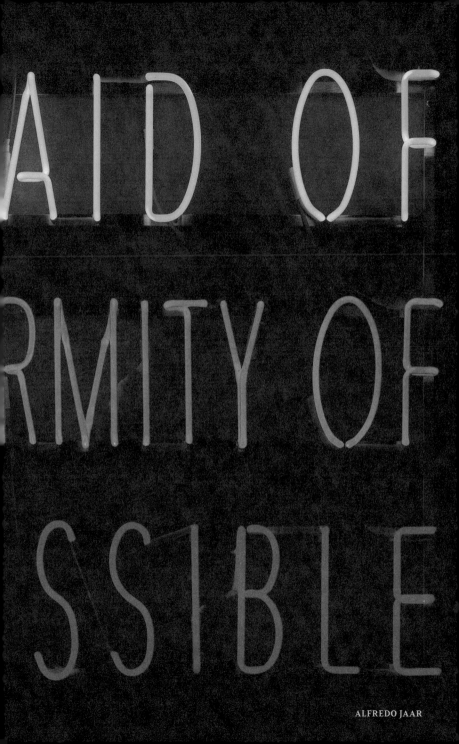

ALFREDO JAAR

May

THE 5TH MONTH | 31 DAYS

Milk Moon – MAY

Named for the rich and abundant milk of animals eating fresh May growth.

	SUNDAY	MONDAY	TUESDAY	WEDNESDAY	THURSDAY	FRIDAY	SATURDAY
				1	**2**	**3**	**4**
☼				5:54 am	5:52 am	5:51 am	5:50 am
☼				7:52 pm	7:53 pm	7:54 pm	7:55 pm
◇				13:58:45	14:01:03	14:03:19	14:05:33
☾				2:32 am	3:05 am	3:33 am	3:58 am
☾				12:10 pm	1:26 pm	2:42 pm	3:57 pm
				≈ Aquarius	≈ Aquarius	♓ Pisces	♓ Pisces
	5	**6**	**7**	**8**	**9**	**10**	**11**
☼	5:49 am	5:47 am	5:46 am	5:45 am	5:44 am	5:43 am	5:42 am
☼	7:56 pm	7:57 pm	7:58 pm	7:59 pm	8:00 pm	8:01 pm	8:02 pm
◇	14:07:47	14:09:58	14:12:08	14:14:17	14:16:23	14:18:28	14:20:31
☾	4:22 am	4:46 am	5:14 am	5:46 am	6:25 am	7:12 am	8:09 am
☾	5:13 pm	6:31 pm	7:49 pm	9:08 pm	10:22 pm	11:29 pm	
	♈ Aries	♈ Aries	♉ Taurus	♉ Taurus	♊ Gemini	♊ Gemini	♋ Cancer
	12	**13**	**14**	**15**	**16**	**17**	**18**
☼	5:41 am	5:40 am	5:39 am	5:38 am	5:37 am	5:36 am	5:35 am
☼	8:03 pm	8:04 pm	8:05 pm	8:06 pm	8:07 pm	8:08 pm	8:09 pm
◇	14:22:32	14:24:31	14:26:28	14:28:22	14:30:15	14:32:05	14:33:53
☾	12:24 am	1:08 am	1:43 am	2:10 am	2:33 am	2:54 am	3:13 am
☾	9:12 am	10:18 am	11:24 am	12:28 pm	1:29 pm	2:30 pm	3:29 pm
	♋ Cancer	♌ Leo	♌ Leo	♌ Leo	♍ Virgo	♍ Virgo	♎ Libra

19
- ☼ 5:35 am
- ☼ 8:10 pm
- ☼↔ 14:35:39
- ☽ 3:31 am
- ☾ 4:30 pm
- ♎ Libra

20
- ☼ 5:34 am
- ☼ 8:11 pm
- ☼↔ 14:37:22
- ☽ 3:51 am
- ☾ 5:32 pm
- ♎ Libra

21
- ☼ 5:33 am
- ☼ 8:12 pm
- ☼↔ 14:39:03
- ☽ 4:13 am
- ☾ 6:36 pm
- ♏ Scorpio

22
- ☼ 5:32 am
- ☼ 8:13 pm
- ☼↔ 14:40:41
- ☽ 4:38 am
- ☾ 7:44 pm
- ♏ Scorpio

23
- ☼ 5:31 am
- ☼ 8:14 pm
- ☼↔ 14:42:17
- ☽ 5:09 am
- ☾ 8:52 pm
- ♐ Sagittarius

24
- ☼ 5:31 am
- ☼ 8:15 pm
- ☼↔ 14:43:50
- ☽ 5:48 am
- ☾ 9:58 pm
- ♐ Sagittarius

25
- ☼ 5:30 am
- ☼ 8:15 pm
- ☼↔ 14:45:20
- ☽ 6:38 am
- ☾ 10:59 pm
- ♐ Sagittarius

26
- ☼ 5:29 am
- ☼ 8:16 pm
- ☼↔ 14:46:48
- ☽ 7:38 am
- ☾ 11:51 pm
- ♑ Capricorn

27
- ☼ 5:29 am
- ☼ 8:17 pm
- ☼↔ 14:48:12
- ☽ 8:47 am
- ♑ Capricorn

28
- ☼ 5:28 am
- ☼ 8:18 pm
- ☼↔ 14:49:34
- ☽ 12:33 am
- ☾ 10:01 am
- ♒ Aquarius

29
- ☼ 5:28 am
- ☼ 8:19 pm
- ☼↔ 14:50:53
- ☽ 1:07 am
- ☾ 11:16 am
- ♒ Aquarius

30
- ☼ 5:27 am
- ☼ 8:19 pm
- ☼↔ 14:52:09
- ☽ 1:36 am
- ☾ 12:31 pm
- ♓ Pisces

31
- ☼ 5:27 am
- ☼ 8:20 pm
- ☼↔ 14:53:21
- ☽ 2:01 am
- ☾ 1:44 pm
- ♓ Pisces

Key

SUNRISE	SUNSET	DAY LENGTH	MOONRISE	MOONSET
☼	☼↔	☼↕	☾	☽

May

MONTHLY COLUMNS

Astrology

Happy May 2024. May is a month of miracles, magic, and maturity, a month of warming weather and blooming flowers. Embrace all the earthy comfort and stability brought on by the stylish Sun in Taurus—the sign of values, money, and material possessions—from May 1 until May 20. While some may find that the astrological influences of the Bull are best spent enjoying picnics in the park, visiting your favorite hiking trail, or soaking your worries away in an herbal bath, don't overdo it. Remember: when it comes to Taurus energy, consistency is key, and less is more. If looking for the best period to begin saving for a new investment, increase your income, or treat yourself to a sensual outing, the Taurus New Moon on May 7 is a great time to start. As the month progresses, you may feel more grounded and connected to your fundamental needs, making it easier to focus on your short-term goals, especially once Mercury—the planet of logic—begins a new journey in tactical Taurus on May 15. Keep in mind, your cravings for new experiences and social connections may expand on May 20, May 23, and May 25, when the Sun, Venus, and Jupiter enter chatty Gemini. Get out and explore!

Phenology Calendar

Plan your summer. Who knows if any of it will happen, but planning it seems like an act of self-care. You'll start getting toxic targeted ads for bikini season, getting in shape, fake tanning products. Everything is thriving and multiplying. Deer are having babies, Canada geese chicks are hatching. You can see them marching in a row around Sunset Park.

Herbal Tips

MUGWORT

Mugwort is associated with the zodiac sign of Pisces, which falls between February 19th and March 20th. As an herb, mugwort is known for its calming and grounding effects on the mind and body, and it helps to enhance spiritual practices and intuition.

Pisces is a water sign, and mugwort is associated with the element of water. This means that it is believed to enhance emotional receptivity and the ability to connect with one's emotions, which is said to be a key trait of those born under Pisces. Additionally, mugwort is traditionally used for spiritual and divinatory purposes, and Pisces is considered to be a spiritual and mystical sign. Mugwort is also believed to help with dream work and lucid dreaming. This month, navigate the deep realms of your dreams or the flowing waves of your emotions with mugwort tea, tincture, or hydrosol.

Alligator Mama

LILY CONSUELO SAPORTA TAGIURI

When my mother was eight months pregnant with me, she and my father took a trip to the Okefenokee swamp in Georgia, an almost prehistoric wetland landscape whose name in Hitchiti means "bubbling water" or "trembling earth." The tannic water is tinted almost black like a milkless tea. It is filled with life, most prevalently floating white water lilies and basking obsidian alligators. At eight months pregnant, hardly able to do more than float, my mother slithered into the water to swim alongside her favorite animals, the alligators. Watching from shore, my father worried it might truly be the end for her, pregnant amongst those ancient lethal reptiles. He realized he had to join her.

Like most wild mothers, whose lack of maternal comfort is compensated by their freeness, my mother is persuasive. When my mom

> **"At eight months pregnant, hardly able to do more than float, my mother slithered into the water to swim alongside her favorite animals, the alligators."**

wanted to return to her favorite swamp for her seventieth birthday, my cousin and I agreed to go along. I pictured my mother leaping joyously into the dark water, one with the alligators, her cobalt blue eyes—unafraid and beaming—meeting the alligators' yellow ones.

Together, the lush southern magnolias, pipe-like carnivorous orchids, blue-eyed grass, and Spanish moss dripping from the trees all make an enchanting and eerie landscape. Our plastic kayaks, once we'd slipped into the water, suddenly felt very thin. Past the mangrove-buttressed roots and water irises, the last human we saw warned us of the alligators, in particular their numerousness. "Just be sure to keep all your digits in the boat."

how much lower on the food chain I was compared to this mass of muscle and teeth. I've never felt so edible. It was somehow embarrassing that I was so afraid. Even though I am generally pretty fearless, I hadn't inherited this particular bravery from my mother. But as we saw more and more alligators, and spent time in their home, their confident movement started to feel more majestic than chilling.

Due to the soft ground, this swamp was never cultivated, and unlike the surrounding areas, it was spared from being turned into plantations. For this reason, it doesn't have the same haunting sensation of the areas that surround it; instead, it has the tone of a past geologic period. The landscape delights a part of me that would

I was on edge. The rims of giant lily pads ruffled like the ridges of alligators' backs, the plants' roots hard and coarse as alligator skin. The first alligator I saw was like a sickening illusion, two bumps followed by a rough patch of water. As it came towards me, locking eyes, I saw how massive it was. My blood chilled knowing

like to think the world is partially untouched or that our human behaviors are not of consequence here. It is a naive hope, but the undeveloped quality of the swamp allows me to suspend disbelief. I imagine for a brief moment that here, where the endless miles of paved roads stop, so does our influence. I put on the radio the other day to a news report about the vulnerability of ecosystems, as evidenced by a declining reptilian population. It made me sympathize with these giant, fiercely built alligators, and note their vulnerability. To be alive now, while plants and

imagine my grandparents emerging out of the war and the concentration camps and making their way into the Jim Crow South, from one hateful society into another. Yet they intimately many. My grandfather built the house my aunt lives in, the white and blue stucco a reference of longing for Greece, with a gold coin buried in the ground below the foundation for luck. In lieu of religion, superstitions are the unwavering rules my mother's family follows. Alligators have entered the symbolic realm of superstition. My mother's room is filled with

> **"To be alive now, while plants and animals die off around us, is to be in a state of constant heartbreak.**

animals die off around us, is to be in a state of constant heartbreak. Surrounded by the alligators and my mom's joy, I savored our coexistence.

The South has always felt foreign to me, even though it was where my grandparents settled and mostly raised my aunt and mother. While leading architectural tours of the Acropolis in Athens, Greece, my grandfather—a young, energetic architect who would spearfish in the Piraeus Harbor before work—charmed a couple who eventually helped him get a job at Georgia Tech in Atlanta. It is hard to

> **Surrounded by the alligators and my mom's joy, I savored our coexistence."**

little alligator figurines in between botánica potions and evil eye medallions that ward off some badness, or perhaps call something else in.

Back at the swamp, my mother was itching to get in the water, but somehow we convinced her to wait until the next day. At the motel that night, we turned on the television to a show called *Something Bit Me*. The man onscreen was missing part of an arm. He told a story about swimming in

knew how to create safety in community. They were advocates for peace and active members of the civil rights movement. Their home became a safe, joyful refuge for

an alligator-filled swamp with his friends as a kid and the experience of nearly drowning when a disturbed alligator clamped down on his soft arm. Different alligator experts weighed in with alligator facts. We learned that alligator jaws work like an engineered clamp triggered by the tongue—as soon as you touch it, getting free is nearly impossible. We learned that alligators will take their prey underwater and sit there for hours until the prey

but she didn't want to go swimming anymore. Surprisingly, I felt more disappointed than relieved. I felt like swimming with the alligators would have shrouded us in some super power. Driving the stretch of asphalt away from the swamp, steam rose from the

hot ground and cloaked us in mist. None of us were ready to leave, so we pulled over and walked to the swampy roadside, rain cooling our bodies. Surrounded by sarracenias, my mother plucked us some sweet grass to chew on while we listened to the dense rhythmic hum of insects. She lowered herself onto her stomach, face to face with the plants, grinning, her stance and perspective mirroring that of the alligators.

drowns. We learned that there is no reasoning with them, and that splashing water at them is seen as a challenge they will rise to. My stomach hurt imagining having to swim with them in the morning. My cousin laughed and asked my mother, "You still want to swim with them, Tati Elena?"

By some stroke of luck, it was raining in the morning. Usually that wouldn't stop my mother,

"I felt like swimming with the alligators would have shrouded us in some super power."

Meissen Pump

FRANCESCA DIMATTIO

Pump III

FRANCESCA DIMATTIO

June

THE 6TH MONTH | 30 DAYS

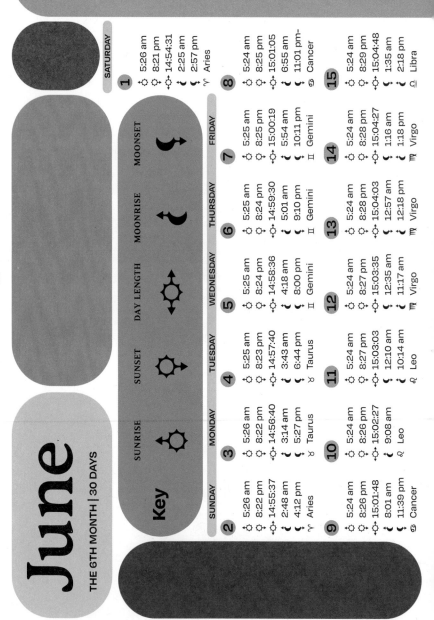

Key

SUNRISE	SUNSET	DAY LENGTH	MOONRISE	MOONSET
☀	☀→	☀↕	☽	☾

SUNDAY	MONDAY	TUESDAY	WEDNESDAY	THURSDAY	FRIDAY	SATURDAY
						1 ☼ 5:26 am / ☼ 8:21 pm / ☼ 14:54:31 / ☽ 2:25 am / ☾ 2:57 pm / ♈ Aries
2 ☼ 5:26 am / ☼ 8:22 pm / ☼ 14:55:37 / ☽ 2:48 am / ☾ 4:12 pm / ♈ Aries	**3** ☼ 5:26 am / ☼ 8:22 pm / ☼ 14:56:40 / ☽ 3:14 am / ☾ 5:27 pm / ♉ Taurus	**4** ☼ 5:25 am / ☼ 8:23 pm / ☼ 14:57:40 / ☽ 3:43 am / ☾ 6:44 pm / ♉ Taurus	**5** ☼ 5:25 am / ☼ 8:24 pm / ☼ 14:58:36 / ☽ 4:18 am / ☾ 8:00 pm / ♊ Gemini	**6** ☼ 5:25 am / ☼ 8:24 pm / ☼ 14:59:30 / ☽ 5:01 am / ☾ 9:10 pm / ♊ Gemini	**7** ☼ 5:25 am / ☼ 8:25 pm / ☼ 15:00:19 / ☽ 5:54 am / ☾ 10:11 pm / ♊ Gemini	**8** ☼ 5:24 am / ☼ 8:25 pm / ☼ 15:01:05 / ☽ 6:55 am / ☾ 11:01 pm– / ♋ Cancer
9 ☼ 5:24 am / ☼ 8:26 pm / ☼ 15:01:48 / ☽ 8:01 am / ☾ 11:39 pm / ♋ Cancer	**10** ☼ 5:24 am / ☼ 8:26 pm / ☼ 15:02:27 / ☽ 9:08 am / ♌ Leo	**11** ☼ 5:24 am / ☼ 8:27 pm / ☼ 15:03:03 / ☽ 12:10 am / ☾ 10:14 am / ♌ Leo	**12** ☼ 5:24 am / ☼ 8:27 pm / ☼ 15:03:35 / ☽ 12:35 am / ☾ 11:17 am / ♍ Virgo	**13** ☼ 5:24 am / ☼ 8:28 pm / ☼ 15:04:03 / ☽ 12:57 am / ☾ 12:18 pm / ♍ Virgo	**14** ☼ 5:24 am / ☼ 8:28 pm / ☼ 15:04:27 / ☽ 1:16 am / ☾ 1:18 pm / ♍ Virgo	**15** ☼ 5:24 am / ☼ 8:29 pm / ☼ 15:04:48 / ☽ 1:35 am / ☾ 2:18 pm / ♎ Libra

16
- ☼ 5:24 am
- ☼ 8:29 pm
- ☼☼ 15:05:06
- ☾ 1:54 am
- ☾ 3:19 pm
- ♎ Libra

17
- ☼ 5:24 am
- ☼ 8:29 pm
- ☼☼ 15:05:19
- ☾ 2:15 am
- ☾ 4:22 pm
- ♏ Scorpio

18
- ☼ 5:24 am
- ☼ 8:30 pm
- ☼☼ 15:05:29
- ☾ 2:39 am
- ☾ 5:28 pm
- ♏ Scorpio

19
- ☼ 5:24 am
- ☼ 8:30 pm
- ☼☼ 15:05:35
- ☾ 3:07 am
- ☾ 6:36 pm
- ♏ Scorpio

20
- ☼ 5:24 am
- ☼ 8:30 pm
- ☼☼ 15:05:38
- ☾ 3:43 am
- ☾ 7:44 pm
- ♐ Sagittarius

21
- ☼ 5:25 am
- ☼ 8:30 pm
- ☼☼ 15:05:36
- ☾ 4:29 am
- ☾ 8:49 pm
- ♐ Sagittarius

22
- ☼ 5:25 am
- ☼ 8:30 pm
- ☼☼ 15:05:31
- ☾ 5:27 am
- ☾ 9:45 pm
- ♑ Capricorn

23
- ☼ 5:25 am
- ☼ 8:31 pm
- ☼☼ 15:05:23
- ☾ 6:34 am
- ☾ 10:31 pm
- ♑ Capricorn

24
- ☼ 5:26 am
- ☼ 8:31 pm
- ☼☼ 15:05:10
- ☾ 7:49 am
- ☾ 11:08 pm
- ♒ Aquarius

25
- ☼ 5:26 am
- ☼ 8:31 pm
- ☼☼ 15:04:54
- ☾ 9:05 am
- ☾ 11:39 pm
- ♒ Aquarius

26
- ☼ 5:26 am
- ☼ 8:31 pm
- ☼☼ 15:04:54
- ☾ 10:21 am
- ♓ Pisces

27
- ☼ 5:27 am
- ☼ 8:31 pm
- ☼☼ 15:04:11
- ☾ 12:05 am
- ☾ 11:35 am
- ♓ Pisces

28
- ☼ 5:27 am
- ☼ 8:31 pm
- ☼☼ 15:03:44
- ☾ 12:29 am
- ☾ 12:48 pm
- ♈ Aries

29
- ☼ 5:27 am
- ☼ 8:31 pm
- ☼☼ 15:03:13
- ☾ 12:52 am
- ☾ 2:01 pm
- ♈ Aries

30
- ☼ 5:28 am
- ☼ 8:31 pm
- ☼☼ 15:02:39
- ☾ 1:17 am
- ☾ 3:15 pm
- ♈ Aries

Strawberry Moon - JUNE
Named for the strawberries that ripen in June.

June

MONTHLY COLUMNS

SUMMER

You haven't been in school in over a decade, but the last-day-of-school feeling is carved into your brain. Ice cream trucks appear. Horseshoe crabs come ashore to lay eggs at Marine Park and Jamaica Bay—their blood is blue and it's used to make vaccines.

Herbal Tips

ROSE

June is associated with the astrological sign of Gemini, and the plant that represents Gemini is the rose. Gemini is a sign that is associated with communication, intellect, and versatility, and the rose embodies these qualities. It is a flower that is versatile in its uses, as it can be used for perfume, cooking, and medicine. It also symbolizes the duality of Gemini, as it can be both delicate and strong. Its thorns are a reminder of the need to protect oneself through softness. Invite softness into your life with rose, a plant with one of the highest frequencies in the plant kingdom. Place rose petals in your bath, use rose water on your body/face, and drink rose tea to access the magic of unconditional love.

Astrology

As June begins and the summer heat approaches, you'll experience a fresh wave of inspiration as Mercury—the planet of learning and self-expression—returns to its home sign, lively Gemini, on June 3. On the plus side, this inquisitive planetary placement strengthens your communication abilities and creative interests. Use the multi-faceted Gemini New Moon peaking on June 6 to share your unique creations, start a new hobby, or travel with friends. However, with Mars—the planet of behavior and willpower—in fixed earth sign Taurus from June 9 until July 20, you may notice that you feel more energized this Gemini season when you stick to a simple daily routine. Fortunately, the second half of June brings a calming turn of events as Venus and Mercury enter nurturing Cancer on June 17, followed by the Sun on June 20. With the start of Cancer season officially marking the beginning of summer, take a moment during the first of two Capricorn Full Moons this year on June 21 to meditate on how you've bloomed since the spring equinox on March 19. You'll be grateful for the extra wisdom once Saturn stations retrograde in impressionable Pisces on June 29.

The Other Wardrobe
WHAT NEXT?

It's better not to wear clothes in summer unless you live in a society, in which case my advice is to always be wearing at least one of the following: undershirts, bike shorts, long dresses with tall slits. I like cotton, but you might like quick-dry. In general try to forget your clothes, though. Summer is the season for accessories. Wear all your necklaces to the beach. That stupid tiny plastic purse you've been wanting to use will look kind of chilled out if you wear it with shorts.

Summer is a good time to daydream about what you might wear when clothes become relevant again. The Aughts' candy-coated business casual (2000s does 1930s' shorthander/typist) is in our current Aughts nostalgia run resurrected in the New Lady look. Her shoes are pointed. Her heel is low, if at all. Her hems skim the ankle or wrist, or, for summer, cut wide across the elbow. It's Edwardian proportions. Waists are so high as to be low. The empire waists of French Democracy's Hellenistic gowns are reprised in their role by pants that feature two or more waistbands, with one high-waisted and the other low-waisted, or by revealing the high elastic waists of hosiery underneath a low-slung skirt. In bodily terms this means the tummy or the torso is its own third zone, starting below the "top," yet also somehow hauntingly contiguous with the "bottom." And each waistband its own resting place.

Waistbands, belts, pockets and other load-bearing elements will continue to receive special decorative focus as continued desire for function and comfort drives innovation in this infamously unaccommodating technology. Partly I think this is about the womb, but it's also about the bladder, the guts, the stomach, the desire to give room to our soft bellies, to carry the weight low, on our thighs, to say *yes I carry this weight, it has pockets and the pockets are BIG* (see Miu Miu SS23, look 56). At the same time it (it being both double waistbands generally and Miu Miu's styling specifically) recalls the practice of sagging, where the waistbands of pants and underwear are both visible.

Haitian Griot & Pikliz

ANDREW CENEUS

Ingredients

GRIOT

- 3 pounds pork shoulder, cubed
- Salt, to taste
- ½ teaspoon freshly cracked pepper, to taste
- 1 onion, chopped
- 2 shallots, chopped
- 5 scallions, chopped
- 1 bell pepper, sliced
- 6 cloves garlic, sliced
- 1 cube chicken bouillon
- 4 cloves garlic
- 2 oranges, juiced
- 2 limes, juiced
- 1 tablespoon white wine

Ingredients

- 10 sprigs fresh thyme
- vinegar
- ½ bunch fresh parsley
- 1 scotch bonnet pepper, sliced
- 2 cups water
- 4 cups oil, for frying
- Brown rice, to serve
- Red bean, to serve
- 3 fried plantains, to serve

PIKLIZ

- 2 cups cabbage, shredded
- 1 cup carrot, grated
- 1 bell pepper, sliced
- 1 onion, sliced
- 3 scallions, sliced
- 1 shallot, sliced
- Salt, to taste
- Pepper, to taste
- 1 scotch bonnet pepper, divided
- 2 cups white wine vinegar

Directions

1. For the griot, add the cubed pork shoulder, salt, pepper, chopped onion, chopped shallots, chopped scallions, sliced bell pepper, sliced garlic, chicken bouillon cube, cloves, orange juice, lime juice, white wine vinegar, thyme sprigs, parsley, and the sliced scotch bonnet pepper to a large dutch oven off the heat. With gloves on, mix the mixture thoroughly. Cover the pot and place in the refrigerator to marinate overnight.

2. For the pikliz, combine the shredded cabbage, grated carrot, 1 sliced bell pepper, 1 sliced onion, 3 sliced scallions, 1 sliced shallot, and 2 sliced scotch bonnet peppers in a large bowl. Add the salt and freshly cracked black pepper.

3. Put on gloves, and thoroughly mix using your hands. Pack the pikliz down into sterilized mason jars. Cover with the white wine vinegar. Put on the lid and store in the refrigerator for at least 12 hours to marinate.

4. Preheat oven to 350°F (180°C). Place the dutch oven with the marinated pork on the stove. Add the 2 cups of water and bring to a boil. Transfer the pork to the oven to braise for 1½ hours or until cooked through and tender. Pick out all the pieces of pork and place on a paper towel-lined tray to dry. Pat down the surface of the pork to make sure there is no moisture.

5. Heat a pot of oil to 350°F (180°C). Add the pork in batches and fry until deep golden brown color, about 5 to 7 minutes. Transfer the pork to a paper towel-lined plate to drain. Serve with rice, beans, fried plantains, and the pikliz.

An Era of Romanticism on Social Media

ANDREA ALISEDA

Romanticism holds a bounty, as an artistic movement originating in the 18th century, an affirmation of love, and a state of being. Whether manifested through escapism or mindfulness, romance is a reckoning with the tempo of life, a meditation of its every moment unfolding like so many rosebuds in the wake of a long-awaited spring.

Like the seasons of nature, in the seasons of life, it is sometimes the bleakness of the world that propels humanity to find a *joie de vivre* as a means of survival.

For the English in the late 18th century, escapism, nostalgia, and mindfulness were tools of rebellion used by the Romantics against the darkness brought on by the Industrial Revolution. The changes of this era decimated human rights and

mother nature; adults and children alike worked long hours in unsanitary and dangerous conditions, while paid too little to live with dignity. The work conditions were so horrendous that, on average, approximately 112 laboring children died and 6,389 were injured daily. But human suffering wasn't industrialism's only toll.

"The advent of mass farming, factories, roads, train lines, and urban sprawl has been a death knell for wild places," writes the English Natural History Museum, "and it was accelerated by the Industrial Revolution in the nineteenth century." Because of this, the UK has now lost over 40 million birds, and half of its natural biodiversity.

Industrialism, later coupled with the year of 1816, known as "the year without a summer"—which occurred from the largest volcanic

eruption in history in modern-day Indonesia, causing skies to darken and climate temperatures to drop across the globe—ushered in the epoch of the Romantics. The widely felt consequences of these turmoils birthed the Romanticism movement, which celebrated communion with nature, cherishing solitude, and honing our individuality and spirituality. Poets and artists like Francisco de Goya, William Wordsworth, Percy Shelley, William Blake, and John Keats sought out a return to nature as industrialization and the volcanic eruption pummeled a world that was quickly fading.

It is from this environment that William Blake penned "The Chimney Sweeper: When my mother died I was very young." In the poem Blake illustrates the bleakness of the times from a child's perspective:

> "When my
> mother died I was
> very young,
> And my father
> sold me while yet
> my tongue
> Could scarcely
> cry" 'weep! 'weep!
> 'weep! 'weep!"
> So your chimneys
> I sweep & in
> soot I sleep."

But in these same times, as the Romantic Period flourished, these pastoral words would become emblematic of it:

> "To swell the
> gourd, and plump
> the hazel shells
> With a sweet
> kernel; to set
> budding more,
> And still more,
> later flowers for
> the bees,
> Until they think
> warm days will
> never cease,
> For summer has
> o'er-brimm'd their
> clammy cells." —
> John Keats,
> "To Autumn"

Romantics romanticized nature and rural life as a response to grief and, in hindsight, as a way to cope.

About 200 years later,

at the start of the global COVID-19 pandemic in 2020, coupled with the George Floyd Uprisings, we began to see the seedlings of Romanticism once again take root. Much like in 18th century England, people longed for a return to rural life, a pastoral dreamscape that would take them out of their pain and suffering into a moment of stillness: greener grass and bluer skies. And these romantic longings evolved through our main medium of communication: social media.

People baked bread from scratch, so much that it caused a flour shortage. "Bread baking is a thing we do in a crisis, perhaps because bread is one of the very foundations of human civilization, and perhaps because it has been marketed to us as life-giving," wrote Emily St. James for Vox in 2020. This marked the beginning of our modern-day romantic era.

Synchronistically, a trend called "cottagecore" arose as a definitive style to encapsulate the times. Cottagecore evokes the same call for simplicity, pastoral nature, and romance through fashion and personal style: wearing petticoats, dresses with puffed sleeves, and corsets.

"Cottagecore, an aesthetic straight out of a laudanum-induced Laura Ingalls Wilder dream, was everywhere: on runways, all over TikTok, in video games, and most notably on Instagram," wrote Shana Shipin for *Glamour* about Black women reclaiming this piece of history through clothing as "ambassadors of the trend."

And it isn't just an aesthetic; this trend has a very definitive lifestyle and universe attached to it: farmers markets, picnics, walks through nature, a good book with a cup of tea.

"It's the same desire for escapism that has people turning to games like Animal Crossing, reverting back to an uncomplicated life of picking fruits and fishing at the river," mused Gabe Bergado in the spring of 2020 for *Teen Vogue*. "Those basic things make sense when much of the world today is confusing, overwhelming, and depressing."

Well into 2023, the darkness still hastens over USians. The uptick in mass shootings continues—there's been 160 so far this year, and by the time this piece publishes, that number is sure to rise. The climate crisis, again, accelerated by the English Industrial Revolution, has continued to cause devastation globally.

The FBI reports that racial hate crimes are on the rise. Rights to abortion have been stripped in twelve states, books are being banned, anti-trans bills continue to be pushed, and robots are edging humans out of work. It remains a dark, overwhelming, and depressing time.

A small choice folks have made to stoke the flames of light has been to romanticize life. We continue to see it on our social channels. Through short-form videos, a sign of our times, viewers and creators alike have embraced the visceral necessity of romance, making the ordinary luxurious, sweet.

Kittie Harloe (@kittieharloe), a singer and content creator "devoted to pleasure wellness and luxury," uses the hashtag #romanticizeyourlife and encourages viewers to engage their senses every day to heighten a sexy and romantic daily experience. Through self-care, fragrance, and house "floozy" duties, Harloe touches again on the Romanticism pillars that focus on individual development and reveling in time with oneself.

Likewise, content creator Barbara Brignoni (@barbiebrignoni) takes to the magic of film to showcase a moment in time poetically in nature and cities alike, exemplifying the joy of being and the joy of nature.

> "Much like in 18th century England, people longed for a return to rural life, a pastoral dreamscape that would take them out of their pain and suffering into a moment of stillness: greener grass and bluer skies."

practices romance, saying in a video, "romanticizing life is about learning to love your everyday—" even, and maybe especially, the quotidian.

Themes that were at the core of English Romanticism—communion with nature, cherishing solitude, honing our individuality and spirituality—live on, resurfacing cyclically, naturally, when needed the most. And in this period filled with so much uncertainty, content creators send viewers the message that it's in our best interest to romanticize the small things—because it's all the small things, the seemingly mundane moments, that add up to a lifetime.

Bethany Ciotola (@bethanyciotola), who looks like a Jane Austen character come-to-life, is another TikTok creator who

Bodybuilder Deities in the Garden

ESTHER ELIA

July
THE 7TH MONTH | 31 DAYS

Buck Moon - JULY
Named for the antlers that start to grow on deer bucks heads.

Key

☀→ SUNRISE

☀→ SUNSET

☀ DAY LENGTH

MONDAY	TUESDAY	WEDNESDAY	THURSDAY	FRIDAY	SATURDAY	SUNDAY
1	**2**	**3**	**4**	**5**	**6**	**7**
☀ 5:28 am	☀ 5:29 am	☀ 5:30 pm	☀ 5:30 am	☀ 5:31 am	☀ 5:31 am	☀ 5:32 am
☀ 8:30 pm	☀ 8:30 pm	☀ 8:30 pm	☀ 8:30 pm	☀ 8:30 pm	☀ 8:29 pm	☀ 8:29 pm
☀ 15:02:01	☀ 15:01:20	☀ 15:00:35	☀ 14:59:46	☀ 14:58:55	☀ 14:58:00	☀ 14:57:01
☽ 1:44 am	☽ 2:16 am	☽ 2:55 am	☽ 3:43 am	☽ 4:41 am	☽ 5:45 am	☽ 6:52 am
☽ 4:30 pm	☽ 5:44 pm	☽ 6:56 pm	☽ 7:59 pm	☽ 8:53 pm	☽ 9:35 pm	☽ 10:09 pm
♉ Taurus	♉ Taurus	♊ Gemini	♊ Gemini	♋ Cancer	♋ Cancer	♌ Leo
8	**9**	**10**	**11**	**12**	**13**	
☀ 5:33 am	☀ 5:33 am	☀ 5:34 am	☀ 5:35 am	☀ 5:35 am	☀ 5:36 am	
☀ 8:29 pm	☀ 8:28 pm	☀ 8:28 pm	☀ 8:27 pm	☀ 8:27 pm	☀ 8:26 pm	
☀ 14:56:00	☀ 14:54:55	☀ 14:53:47	☀ 14:52:35	☀ 14:51:21	☀ 14:50:04	
☽ 7:59 am	☽ 9:04 am	☽ 10:06 am	☽ 11:07 am	☽ 12:06 pm	☽ 1:06 pm	
☽ 10:37 pm	☽ 11:00 pm	☽ 11:20 pm	☽ 11:39 pm	☽ 11:57 pm	☽ Libra	
♌ Leo	♌ Leo	♍ Virgo	♍ Virgo	♎ Libra		

14
☀ 5:37 am
☽ 8:26 pm
☿ 14:48:44
☾ 12:17 am
☾ 2:08 pm
♎ Libra

15
☀ 5:38 am
☽ 8:25 pm
☿ 14:47:21
☾ 12:39 am
☾ 3:12 pm
♏ Scorpio

16
☀ 5:39 am
☽ 8:24 pm
☿ 14:45:55
☾ 1:05 am
☾ 4:19 pm
♏ Scorpio

17
☀ 5:39 am
☽ 8:24 pm
☿ 14:44:26
☾ 1:37 am
☾ 5:27 pm
♐ Sagittarius

18
☀ 5:40 am
☽ 8:23 pm
☿ 14:42:55
☾ 2:18 am
☾ 6:33 pm
♐ Sagittarius

19
☀ 5:41 am
☽ 8:22 pm
☿ 14:41:21
☾ 3:11 am
☾ 7:33 pm
♑ Capricorn

20
☀ 5:42 am
☽ 8:22 pm
☿ 14:39:45
☾ 4:15 am
☾ 8:24 pm
♑ Capricorn

21
☀ 5:43 am
☽ 8:21 pm
☿ 14:38:06
☾ 5:28 am
☾ 9:06 pm
≈ Aquarius

22
☀ 5:44 am
☽ 8:20 pm
☿ 14:36:24
☾ 6:47 am
☾ 9:39 pm
≈ Aquarius

23
☀ 5:44 am
☽ 8:19 pm
☿ 14:34:40
☾ 8:05 am
☾ 10:08 pm
≈ Aquarius

24
☀ 5:45 am
☽ 8:18 pm
☿ 14:32:54
☾ 9:22 am
☾ 10:33 pm
♓ Pisces

25
☀ 5:46 am
☽ 8:17 pm
☿ 14:31:06
☾ 10:38 pm
☾ 10:57 pm
♓ Pisces

26
☀ 5:47 am
☽ 8:16 pm
☿ 14:29:15
☾ 11:52 pm
☾ 11:21 pm
♈ Aries

27
☀ 5:48 am
☽ 8:15 pm
☿ 14:27:23
☾ 1:06 pm
☾ 11:47 pm
♈ Aries

28
☀ 5:49 am
☽ 8:14 pm
☿ 14:25:28
☾ 2:21 pm
♉ Taurus

29
☀ 5:50 am
☽ 8:13 pm
☿ 14:23:31
☾ 12:17 am
☾ 3:35 pm
♉ Taurus

30
☀ 5:51 am
☽ 8:12 pm
☿ 14:21:32
☾ 12:53 am
☾ 4:47 pm
♊ Gemini

31
☀ 5:52 am
☽ 8:11 pm
☿ 14:19:32
☾ 1:38 am
☾ 5:52 pm
♊ Gemini

July

MONTHLY COLUMNS

Astrology

July may be one of the hottest months of the year, but the Sun in watery Cancer until July 20 will help you to be cool, calm, and collected. Keep this in mind on July 2, when sleepy Neptune stations retrograde in peaceful Pisces and chatty Mercury marches into liberating Leo until July 25. These cosmic shifts ask you to tune into your inner power as Neptune retrograde encourages you to establish emotional boundaries, and Mercury in Leo pushes you to communicate with confidence. With the nostalgic Cancer New Moon also occurring a few days later on July 5, July is an excellent month to spend quality time with loved ones and make home improvements. With socialite Venus also in lively Leo from July 11 until August 4, you may be more outgoing this Cancer season than usual. However, with the second and final Capricorn Full Moon of 2024 lighting up the skies on July 21, it's important to prioritize responsibilities before saying yes to risky decisions and expensive purchases!

Herbal Tips

MOTHERWORT

Motherwort has traditionally been used to support the emotional well-being of individuals, especially during times of stress and anxiety. July, being a month of Cancer energy, warrants the big bear hug that motherwort provides. In addition to its emotional support properties, motherwort is also known for its ability to promote heart health and regulate menstrual cycles. This is because it contains compounds that act as a natural sedative and anti-inflammatory agent. The plant has also been used to promote relaxation and aid in sleep, making it an ideal herb for those who struggle with insomnia or restlessness. Overall, motherwort is a beautiful plant that offers a wide range of benefits for both physical and emotional health. Source a motherwort tincture from a trusted herbalist and experience why this comforting plant has the word mother in its name.

Phenology Calendar

It's manageably hot. During the day the air smells like barbeque and at night it smells like gunpowder from fireworks. When you go to Tilden, the sand is blocked off so that Piping Plovers (an endangered species) can lay their eggs and raise their chicks in the summer home they share with you.

Rerooting

KIRK GORDON

The year I was born, my parents planted a pin oak in our yard—a symbol of new life and a gesture toward the future they hoped to create for me. Year after year, the tree and I grew alongside one another. Slowly we began to develop different attitudes towards the soil we were planted in. Like so

"With my own feet now on fertile ground, I find wisdom in this steadfast commitment to place, consulting the trees on matters of patience and persistence."

quiet intelligence allows trees to live hundreds of years in the same spot. The Alley Pond Giant—New York City's oldest tree—was a sapling when the Dutch arrived. It's the only living being to have witnessed the city's development from the beginning. With my own feet now on fertile

many small-town queer kids, I grew up feeling stunted and choked by the inhospitable terrain around me. I kept my roots small and nimble, and when an opportunity finally presented itself, I picked them up and ran east. The oak tree, unable to follow, spread its roots deep and wide, eventually encircling

ground, I find wisdom in this steadfast commitment to place, consulting the trees on matters of patience and persistence. But to fixate too much on this quality of rootedness is to quite literally miss the forest for the trees. While a single oak may stand rooted in place, the forests, my friends, are running.

the foundation of our home.

Such is the reality of arboreal life. Unable to move in the face of adverse conditions, trees have become masters of adaptation in place, regulating nutrient uptake and metabolism to survive dramatic fluctuations in their environment. This

As a landscape architect in New York City, much of my work focuses on adapting our built environment to the challenges of climate change. As weather patterns begin to dramatically shift, many

tree species are moving beyond their native ranges in an effort to keep up. In the eastern United States, hardwoods are moving west, while softwoods like pine and spruce are moving north. Ecosystems are being spliced and reshuffled, as old and familiar neighbors move in opposite directions.

For plant communities, migration is an intergenerational affair. Along the shores of every forest, mature trees cast their offspring outward to be carried by the winds or in the bellies of chirping songbirds. Each wave of young seedlings will eventually rise and crest, spilling more seeds outward and rising yet again. Movement is a communal ritual.

Forests have crept along in this rhythmic fashion, growing across generational tides, for millions of years. During North America's last glacial retreat, pine and spruce trees swept the newly thawed landscape by upwards of a kilometer a

year. Birch, maple, and beech soon followed. Through cycles of adaptation and competition, indigenous stewardship and settler-colonization, these species gradually became the forest communities we know today.

Our contemporary forests possess the same capacity to migrate in the face of climatic shifts, but they face an entirely new challenge: industrial development. Capitalist land use has deeply fragmented the mosaic of otherwise suitable habitat, with waves

of young seedlings now crashing against the cliffs of vast agricultural fields and sprawling suburban development. In forest ecology, there is a term for this inhospitality: the outer seed shadow. In this zone, young seedlings fail to find fertile ground in proximity to their parents, falling victim to disturbances or

"As weather patterns begin to dramatically shift, many tree species are moving beyond their native ranges in an effort to keep up."

environmental pressures and never reaching maturity. Such a fate haunts many human children as well.

For the future of our forests, these complications are the border walls. Certain species, due to their adaptability or seed dispersal method, are better than others at leaping over these walls. But many tree populations face a daunting future, effectively siloed within landscapes that will become too hot or dry for them to survive. As climate change accelerates, some species may not be able to keep up.

To save these vulnerable populations, ecologists have begun to advocate for the idea of "assisted migration"— proactively introducing species where future habitat conditions are projected to be more favorable. This intentional curation of plant communities echoes

centuries of indigenous forest stewardship, and amounts to climate gardening on a regional scale.

Deliberately altering ecosystems carries both rewards and risks, so site selection is key. Growing evidence shows that urban forests—the rectilinear network of trees that braid together our parks and neighborhoods—may play a special role in supporting regional forests long-term. The density of paved surfaces causes cities to absorb more heat than their surroundings, producing a phenomena known as the urban heat island effect. When considering climate change, cities also become islands in time—places where climatic shifts are sped up and exacerbated. The cities of the Atlantic Seaboard represent an archipelago of the future—a string of portals by which to step into the climatic conditions of the coming century.

Our urban forests are at the forefront of climate change, presenting both challenges and opportunities. By replacing declining tree species with more southern-adapted selections, we can incubate early populations of climate-resilient trees in regions where winters are otherwise still too cold. As the rest of the region warms, new seedlings may find ground beyond the city, filling the niche of species that have migrated elsewhere.

Despite these potential advantages, the broad ecological implications of assisted migration leave a lot of questions. Will intentional introduction be helpful, or disruptive? The reality is that, as the climate warms, most ecosystems are in for a shake-up. Having made a home in New York, I will mourn the slow fade of black birch's sweet scent, and the friendly shimmer of trembling aspen. Ecosystems are set to shift and reorganize, and new pairings of species will hybridize, outcompete, and coexist with one another. What strange new combinations might the future hold?

Urban forests offer a creative opportunity to consider this question. Already heavily curated by human hands, urban ecosystems exist as artificial compositions of species that would not naturally cohabitate. They're one big garden—a living mosaic of a thousand tiny actions by communities to create a sense of place. As the climate changes and our cities transform around us, we must embrace the strange new worlds that become possible. Perhaps one day we will kayak through the bald cypress swamps of Staten Island, or picnic in the sourwood-magnolia groves in north Baltimore. What new places might begin to feel like home?

When I visit the tree my parents planted in our yard years ago, I wonder what kind of future they had envisioned. The pin oak, having never moved away, has grown much taller than me. Native to areas further south, it's projected to do quite well in my home state over the next century. The future will carry stories that exceed our imaginations. In the gaps between reality and expectations, we may find the most fertile ground.

> **"Having made a home in New York, I will mourn the slow fade of black birch's sweet scent, and the friendly shimmer of trembling aspen."**

Boombox

10TH FLOOR STUDIO

August

THE 8TH MONTH | 31 DAYS

Key

SUNRISE	SUNSET	DAY LENGTH	MOONRISE	MOONSET

Sturgeon Moon - AUGUST
Named for the time of year when sturgeons are most abundant in lakes.

SUNDAY	MONDAY	TUESDAY	WEDNESDAY	THURSDAY	FRIDAY	SATURDAY
				1	**2**	**3**
				☼ 5:53 am	☼ 5:54 am	☼ 5:55 am
				☼ 8:10 pm	☼ 8:09 pm	☼ 8:08 pm
				☼ 14:17:29	☼ 14:15:25	☼ 14:13:19
				☾ 2:32 am	☾ 3:33 am	☾ 4:39 am
				☾ 6:48 pm	☾ 7:33 pm	☾ 8:10 pm
				♋ Cancer	♋ Cancer	♌ Leo
4	**5**	**6**	**7**	**8**	**9**	**10**
☼ 5:56 am	☼ 5:57 am	☼ 5:58 am	☼ 5:59 am	☼ 6:00 am	☼ 6:01 am	☼ 6:02 am
☼ 8:07 pm	☼ 8:06 pm	☼ 8:04 pm	☼ 8:03 pm	☼ 8:02 pm	☼ 8:01 pm	☼ 7:59 pm
☼ 14:11:11	☼ 14:09:02	☼ 14:06:51	☼ 14:04:38	☼ 14:02:25	☼ 14:00:09	☼ 13:57:53
☾ 5:46 am	☾ 6:52 am	☾ 7:55 am	☾ 8:56 am	☾ 9:56 am	☾ 10:55 am	☾ 11:56 am
☾ 8:39 pm	☾ 9:03 pm	☾ 9:24 pm	☾ 9:43 pm	☾ 10:01 pm	☾ 10:20 pm	☾ 10:41 pm
♌ Leo	♌ Leo	♍ Virgo	♍ Virgo	♎ Libra	♎ Libra	♎ Libra

11	**12**	**13**	**14**	**15**	**16**	**17**
☼ 6:03 am	☼ 6:04 am	☼ 6:04 am	☼ 6:05 am	☼ 6:06 am	☼ 6:07 am	☼ 6:08 am
☼ 7:58 pm	☼ 7:57 pm	☼ 7:55 pm	☼ 7:54 pm	☼ 7:53 pm	☼ 7:51 pm	☼ 7:50 pm
☼☼ 13:55:35	☼☼ 13:53:16	☼☼ 13:50:56	☼☼ 13:48:35	☼☼ 13:46:12	☼☼ 13:43:49	☼☼ 13:41:24
☾ 12:58 pm	☾ 2:03 pm	☾ 3:09 pm	☾ 4:16 pm	☾ 5:18 pm	☾ 1:54 am	☾ 3:03 am
☾ 11:05 pm	☾ 11:34 pm	☾	☾	☾	☾ 6:13 pm	☾ 6:58 pm
♏ Scorpio	♏ Scorpio	♐ Sagittarius	♐ Sagittarius	♐ Sagittarius	♑ Capricorn	♑ Capricorn

18	**19**	**20**	**21**	**22**	**23**	**24**
☼ 6:09 am	☼ 6:10 am	☼ 6:11 am	☼ 6:12 am	☼ 6:13 am	☼ 6:14 am	☼ 6:15 am
☼ 7:48 pm	☼ 7:47 pm	☼ 7:45 pm	☼ 7:44 pm	☼ 7:42 pm	☼ 7:41 pm	☼ 7:39 pm
☼☼ 13:38:59	☼☼ 13:36:33	☼☼ 13:34:06	☼☼ 13:31:38	☼☼ 13:29:09	☼☼ 13:26:39	☼☼ 13:24:09
☾ 4:20 am	☾ 5:40 am	☾ 6:59 am	☾ 8:18 am	☾ 9:35 am	☾ 10:52 am	☾ 12:09 pm
☾ 7:36 pm	☾ 8:07 pm	☾ 8:34 pm	☾ 8:58 pm	☾ 9:23 pm	☾ 9:49 pm	☾ 10:18 pm
♒ Aquarius	♒ Aquarius	♓ Pisces	♓ Pisces	♈ Aries	♈ Aries	♉ Taurus

25	**26**	**27**	**28**	**29**	**30**	**31**
☼ 6:16 am	☼ 6:17 am	☼ 6:18 am	☼ 6:19 am	☼ 6:20 am	☼ 6:21 am	☼ 6:22 am
☼ 7:38 pm	☼ 7:36 pm	☼ 7:35 pm	☼ 7:33 pm	☼ 7:32 pm	☼ 7:30 pm	☼ 7:28 pm
☼☼ 13:21:37	☼☼ 13:19:06	☼☼ 13:16:33	☼☼ 13:14:00	☼☼ 13:11:26	☼☼ 13:08:52	☼☼ 13:06:17
☾ 1:25 pm	☾ 2:39 pm	☾ 3:47 pm	☾ 12:26 am	☾ 1:25 am	☾ 2:30 am	☾ 3:36 am
☾ 10:53 pm	☾ 11:35 pm	☾	☾ 4:45 pm	☾ 5:33 pm	☾ 6:12 pm	☾ 6:42 pm
♉ Taurus	♊ Gemini	♊ Gemini	♋ Cancer	♋ Cancer	♋ Cancer	♌ Leo

August

Phenology Calendar

In August, you can see monarch butterflies fluttering around in pollinator gardens, meadows, and open fields where late summer-blooming wildflowers grow. Therapists go on vacation in August, so people will be stressed and bottled up and sweaty. Avoid the subway, if you can—the feeling of another person's sweat on the back of your arms can send anyone into a mental breakdown.

Herbal Tips

CALENDULA

Leo is represented by the lion, a symbol of strength, courage, and vitality. Calendula is believed to embody these qualities and is associated with the sun, which is also connected to the sign of Leo. Calendula is a vibrant and powerful herb that is often used for its medicinal properties. It has an affinity for the skin, making it a popular ingredient in ointments, creams, and salves. The most common ways to use calendula besides healing skincare products are:

1. Tea: Dried calendula flowers can be steeped in hot water to make tea, which has anti-inflammatory & antioxidant properties. It can also help improve digestion and boost the immune system.

2. Bath: Adding calendula flowers to your bath water can help improve skin health, soothe minor skin irritations, and promote relaxation.

3. Oil infusion: You can infuse calendula flowers to create a natural oil that can be used for skincare or massage. Calendula oil can also be added to homemade candles or soap for added benefits.

This sun-filled plant is a multi-purpose herb that can be used in a variety of ways to promote wellness and beauty.

Astrology

August 2024 is a month of refinement and reorganization. For starters, August begins on a groundbreaking note as the heart-opening New Moon in Leo reaches its peak on August 4. During this transit, childhood passions and a desire for romance will come to the forefront of the collective. However, keep in mind that Mercury will be retrograde in practical Virgo from August 5 until August 14, and in pleasure-seeking Leo from August 14 until August 28, so you may need to review your grand plans and love interests before taking them mainstream. Luckily, the Aquarius Full Moon on April 19 offers the community support you need to understand and elevate your efforts. With Aquarius ruling groups and cultural adaption, you may experience changes to a team project or within your friendship circle. While things may be temporarily sluggish with Mercury retrograde for most of the month, expect a change of pace on August 22, when the Sun slips into industrious Virgo. During this transit, it may be best to incorporate more relaxation into your daily routines to prevent burnout. Self-care will become especially important once Venus enters Libra on August 29.

Red Water

DYLAN SMITH

By the end of August I'd left the city to help some friends renovate an old yellow farmhouse in Olivebridge, New York. The house was on fifty acres of farmable land a half-hour south of the Ashokan Reservoir, which supplies New York City with 40% of its water. If you helped renovate the house you could sleep on a mat in their attic for free. The air was deep blue green up there in the summertime. But this was in 2020. Everybody was freaking out. After you renovated the house, my friends made you pay for a room.

To make rent I worked for this wild old woodsman up there by the reservoir. He was full of memory, full of wild numbers. We drove around the reservoir in his van drinking beer. The city uses a billion gallons of water a day, the old man told me. An olympic pool per minute. That's 680,000 gallons, he said. What's 40% of that? The old man added an extra sound to the word water. Imagine it, he said: 272,000 gallons of *worter*.

The Ashokan Reservoir is ninety-something miles north of the city. Eight thousand blue acres big. The old man told me about eminent domain, which in this case allowed the New York City Board of Water Supply to forcibly evict, then flood eleven mountain towns between 1907 and 1915. Over 2,300 people lost their homes, their big red barns and schools, their favorite trees and churches. Even graveyards got dug up.

Now cops in cars guard the man-made water. If you ever go up there you'll notice them. NYPD all along the reservoir's upper basin to the west, where the water enters, and down along its lower basin to the east, where it leaves. A weir bridge divides the blue water. Cop cars idle everywhere. The old man told me they're the Department of Environmental Protection. A city force created to police the labor camps when the reservoir was being built. That's the predictable history of the DEP police. They even have their own detective bureau now.

But it wouldn't take much to contaminate the reservoir, the old man said. The reservoir is vulnerable to an attack.

It's all just right there—40% of the city's *worter*.

Nobody I lived with liked to talk about it much, but the well water at the farmhouse got everybody sick. That's the wild thing about living so close to the reservoir— everybody up there relies on a well, and there are parasites alive in the water.

The farmhouse well was up the hill a little, beside a trickling creek with some trees. From there you looked down on the farmhouse and at this century-old red hay barn. A guy I grew up with named Chris poured a gallon of bleach down the well. I watched him do it beside this big dead maple tree. Chris went around warning everybody. We just shocked the well, Chris said. The water stank like bleach for a bit. Later Chris installed this ultraviolet bulb, which was supposed to kill bacteria with its radiant lavender light. The water tasted alright for a while. But in spring that big dead red maple tree fell onto the well and cracked its concrete lid, and all these frogs and other plague-themed beasts leapt into the hole and died in our water.

Poor Chris. I watched him shock the well again. *Glug glug glug*. But nothing worked. The water fell out of the faucet all pink yellow red and tasted like rocks. Then the barn burnt down. A big red mountain of fire in the middle of the night. I wasn't there. I'd left New York to dry out. Chris said the fire felt astral. Like something out of the bible or the tarot. A fire engine came with 5,000 gallons of water. We didn't feel like kids anymore after that. Nothing Chris tried ever worked. The farmhouse water still gets everybody sick.

The city's water doesn't get filtered either. Like water from the farmhouse well, it gets treated with UV light and bleach. But it also gets fluoride and phosphoric acid added to it. This happens in treatment facilities like the Catskill-Delaware Water Ultraviolet Disinfection Facility in Westchester. It treats two billion gallons of water a day and if anything were to happen, it has a backup supply of treated water that would last the city just two weeks. It's the largest UV treatment facility in the world.

But now we're back in the van with that old man. We're driving around the reservoir again, and he's going on and on about the water tumbling down a 92-mile aqueduct to the city. There are two watersheds that supply the city with *worter*. Two aqueducts. Ours is called the Catskill Aqueduct. The other one is the Delaware— it's the longest aqueduct in the world. Have you ever siphoned gasoline out of a van? That's how the

aqueducts work. The old man told me to think of them as huge subterranean hoses. But no pumps or anything. Just gravity pushing and pulling at a billion gallons of water.

For the first half of 2024, the Delaware Aqueduct will need to be shut down. Apparently it leaks. Tens of millions of gallons of water into the bedrock beneath the Hudson River every day. Workers already built a three-mile diversion tunnel around the leak, the old man told me. But the Delaware Aqueduct will need to be blocked up until they can reconnect it. The old man told me it's a really big deal. If you're reading this in the first six-or-so months of 2024, the Ashokan Reservoir is essentially the sole source of New York City's water.

In 2020 I read a lot about radical attempts at revolution in America.

The Weather Underground. The legacy of Bernardine Dohrn.

Probably nobody should contaminate the city's water supply. But seriously—somebody could. Those DEP cops must be freaking out.

This last part happened just the other day. I'm on a date in the city drinking water. I live here now. The barn-red doors of an FDNY building open and close and open and close and open, and I'm sober again. It's one of those sparkling rare astral moments when everything behind you is behind you, and everything before you is before you,

and everything inside you is aligning. The person I'm with got sick from the farmhouse water too. We're sitting at this table talking about the warming earth and poems, revolutions, and we're marveling at how the city still sends out red trucks full of people into traffic to fight fires using *worter*. I don't think anybody should contaminate the reservoir. My date touches my hand and laughs. I forget for a minute that everything is fucked. My eyes well up with water. It feels incredible. I am in love.

Blood Is Always Red

JENNIFER GIVHAN

The way light must penetrate our skin
as sunlight through the atmosphere
asks us to imagine we beat magenta or berry
jam, sangria, blackberry wine.
Harder to swallow perhaps are those
who swear that if you sliced us
open, only then would the gush of air
turn what streams from our veins
from teal or sapphire or navy to
the color we see in the streets.
The way I have held this space for my babies—
nearly grown—taller than me by a foot
or breasted already, and, yes, bleeding
each month both the curse and gift.
And in this space I have believed in prayer candles
burning. My darlings what is love but risk
that we never empty of the magick
or science or the imaginary binding us together
even when we're split by particles. By eternities.
What separation can there be when in this brief
and glorious moment, you are sealed tight
and can explore, in these bodies, everything—
O beautiful creatures I have made or dreamed up—
when the light hits just so. Your blood looks almost like sky.

Carrizo Mountain Dance

TYRRELL TAPAHA

September

THE 9TH MONTH | 30 DAYS

Key

SUNRISE ☼

SUNSET ☼

Harvest Moon - SEPTEMBER

Named for the light that comes from the closeness of the setting sun and rising moon which allows farmers to harvest later into the evening.

SUNDAY	MONDAY	TUESDAY	WEDNESDAY	THURSDAY	FRIDAY	SATURDAY
1 ☼ 6:23 am ☼ 7:27 pm ☼ 13:03:42 ☾ 4:42 am ☾ 7:07 pm ♌ Leo	**2** ☼ 6:24 am ☼ 7:25 pm ☼ 13:01:06 ☾ 5:46 am ☾ 7:29 pm ♍ Virgo	**3** ☼ 6:25 am ☼ 7:24 pm ☼ 12:58:30 ☾ 6:47 am ☾ 7:48 pm ♍ Virgo	**4** ☼ 6:26 am ☼ 7:22 pm ☼ 12:55:53 ☾ 7:47 am ☾ 8:07 pm ♍ Virgo	**5** ☼ 6:27 am ☼ 7:20 pm ☼ 12:53:16 ☾ 8:47 am ☾ 8:25 pm ♎ Libra	**6** ☼ 6:28 am ☼ 7:19 pm ☼ 12:50:38 ☾ 9:47 am ☾ 8:45 pm ♎ Libra	**7** ☼ 6:29 am ☼ 7:17 pm ☼ 12:48:01 ☾ 10:48 am ☾ 9:07 pm ♏ Scorpio
8 ☼ 6:30 am ☼ 7:15 pm ☼ 12:45:22 ☾ 11:52 am ☾ 9:34 pm ♏ Scorpio	**9** ☼ 6:31 am ☼ 7:14 pm ☼ 12:42:44 ☾ 12:57 pm ☾ 10:06 pm ♏ Scorpio	**10** ☼ 6:32 am ☼ 7:12 pm ☼ 12:40:05 ☾ 2:02 pm ☾ 10:47 pm ♐ Sagittarius	**11** ☼ 6:33 am ☼ 7:10 pm ☼ 12:37:26 ☾ 3:04 pm ☾ 11:38 pm ♐ Sagittarius	**12** ☼ 6:34 am ☼ 7:09 pm ☼ 12:34:47 ☾ 4:01 pm ♑ Capricorn	**13** ☼ 6:35 am ☼ 7:07 pm ☼ 12:32:08 ☾ 12:41 am ☾ 4:50 pm ♑ Capricorn	**14** ☼ 6:36 am ☼ 7:05 pm ☼ 12:29:28 ☾ 1:53 am ☾ 5:30 pm ♒ Aquarius

DAY LENGTH ✷ **MOONRISE** ☾ **MOONSET** ☾

15
- ☼ 6:37 am
- ☼ 7:04 pm
- ✷ 12:26:48
- ☾ 3:10 am
- ☾ 6:03 pm
- ≈ Aquarius

16
- ☼ 6:38 am
- ☼ 7:02 pm
- ✷ 12:24:09
- ☾ 4:29 am
- ☾ 6:32 pm
- ✶ Pisces

17
- ☼ 6:39 am
- ☼ 7:00 pm
- ✷ 12:21:29
- ☾ 5:49 am
- ☾ 6:58 pm
- ✶ Pisces

18
- ☼ 6:40 am
- ☼ 6:58 pm
- ✷ 12:18:48
- ☾ 7:08 am
- ☾ 7:22 pm
- ♈ Aries

19
- ☼ 6:41 am
- ☼ 6:57 pm
- ✷ 12:16:08
- ☾ 8:27 am
- ☾ 7:48 pm
- ♈ Aries

20
- ☼ 6:42 am
- ☼ 6:55 pm
- ✷ 12:13:28
- ☾ 9:47 am
- ☾ 8:17 pm
- ♉ Taurus

21
- ☼ 6:43 am
- ☼ 6:53 pm
- ✷ 12:10:47
- ☾ 11:06 am
- ☾ 8:50 pm
- ♉ Taurus

22
- ☼ 6:44 am
- ☼ 6:52 pm
- ✷ 12:08:07
- ☾ 12:24 pm
- ☾ 9:31 pm
- ♊ Gemini

23
- ☼ 6:45 am
- ☼ 6:50 pm
- ✷ 12:05:26
- ☾ 1:37 pm
- ☾ 10:20 pm
- ♊ Gemini

24
- ☼ 6:46 am
- ☼ 6:48 pm
- ✷ 12:02:46
- ☾ 2:40 pm
- ☾ 11:18 pm
- ♊ Gemini

25
- ☼ 6:47 am
- ☼ 6:47 pm
- ✷ 12:00:05
- ☾ 3:32 pm
- ♋ Cancer

26
- ☼ 6:48 am
- ☼ 6:45 pm
- ✷ 11:57:24
- ☾ 12:22 am
- ☾ 4:14 pm
- ♋ Cancer

27
- ☼ 6:49 am
- ☼ 6:43 pm
- ✷ 11:54:44
- ☾ 1:28 am
- ☾ 4:46 pm
- ♌ Leo

28
- ☼ 6:50 am
- ☼ 6:42 pm
- ✷ 11:52:03
- ☾ 2:34 am
- ☾ 5:13 pm
- ♌ Leo

29
- ☼ 6:51 am
- ☼ 6:40 pm
- ✷ 11:49:23
- ☾ 3:38 am
- ☾ 5:35 pm
- ♍ Virgo

30
- ☼ 6:52 am
- ☼ 6:38 pm
- ✷ 11:46:43
- ☾ 4:40 am
- ☾ 5:55 pm
- ♍ Virgo

September

FALL

Herbal Tips

SKULLCAP

Skullcap is an herb that has been used for centuries for its medicinal properties. When prepared as a tincture, it can be an effective way to help with nervous tension, anxiety, and insomnia. Here are instructions to make a skullcap tincture:

Ingredients

- Dried skullcap leaves and flowers
- High-proof alcohol (like vodka or rum)

Steps

- Fill a jar with the dried skullcap leaves and flowers, leaving about an inch of space at the top.
- Pour the high-proof alcohol over the herbs, making sure that they are completely covered.
- Close the jar tightly and give it a good shake.
- Place the jar in a dark, cool place, such as a pantry or cupboard, for 4–6 weeks. Shake the jar periodically to mix the herbs and alcohol.
- After 4–6 weeks, strain the liquid through a cheesecloth or fine mesh strainer, discarding the herbs.
- Store the tincture in a glass bottle with a dropper. To use the skullcap tincture, add a few drops to a glass of water or juice and drink it. It can be taken up to three times a day, depending on the desired effect.

The Other Wardrobe

WHAT NEXT?

FALL

Clothes without a body have no meaning. Clothes on a body do have meaning. Suddenly, they have context, purpose, intent. Where are you going? Who will see you there, and how will you feel? Context, purpose, intent. For fall I recommend wool trousers three sizes too large. Pin the excess on one side at the waist, or if you prefer, distribute it across two or more pins. Wear a shirt or a belt that covers the waistband if you want, but a neatly pinned waistband held down by a decorative pin is a nice look in this writer's opinion. Antique diaper pins in steel and sterling silver are affordable, and will have a strong sprung coil that makes them up to the job. Silver will look nice and intentional if you're wearing a crop top or your shirt is too short and shows your tummy when you reach up to scratch your head. Careful not to use a brooch, which has none of the necessary spring and tension. The best thing about pinned pants is you can readjust them throughout the day as your waistline changes, or if you need to take a slow, deep breath.

September in New York is all hustle and bustle. It is a perfect time for watching. In many neighborhoods you can watch college students arrive in droves. You can observe the plumage and peacocking of designers and their exhausted interns from all over the world as they descend on the city for Fashion Week. You can see birds pass through as they migrate to their homes in the South, and you can see monarch butterflies and their new babies as they depart on their 2,100-mile trip to Mexico.

Astrology

Retrograde season is still in full effect this autumn, so don't be discouraged if fall doesn't kick off quite how you envisioned. Instead of resisting the changes coming on September 1 when Pluto stations retrograde in conservative Capricorn and Uranus stations retrograde in stubborn Taurus, allow yourself the space to heal and make amends with the past. With both Taurus and Capricorn being earth signs—known for their connection to the material world—you may need to address lingering financial or professional concerns throughout the month. Fortunately, the Virgo New Moon on September 2 could offer you the necessary resources to improve your circumstances. Whether it's transitioning to a WFH position, reorganizing your budget, or receiving more assistance with chores, don't be afraid to make decisions that support your well-being. This is especially important to remember once Mars is in passive Cancer from September 4 until November 3. While Virgo season is great for increasing efficiency, the Pisces Lunar Eclipse on September 17 is a reminder that you can't be all work and no play. Use the fall equinox and Sun's entrance into Libra on September 22 to get back to you. What sparks your fire?

Haitian Black Rice

ANDREW CENEUS

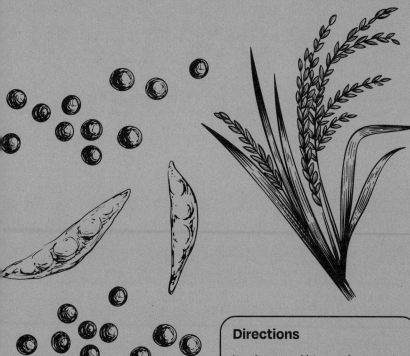

Ingredients

- · 1 cup rice
- · 1 cup dried djon djon OR half of a Maggi cube
- · 1 tablespoon Épis OR Caribbean green seasoning
- · 1 tablespoon butter
- · 2 sprigs thyme
- · 1 stalk scallions
- · 1 tablespoon vegetable seasoning
- · 1 teaspoon Sazon Clasico
- · 1 teaspoon crushed red pepper sauce
- · 1 cup green peas

Directions

1. In a pot, add 4 cups of water to 1 cup of the djon djon and boil it for about 10 minutes. If you'd like to go the traditional route, soak the djon djon overnight. If you aren't able to get djon djon, dissolve half of a Maggi cube in 2 cups of hot water.

2. Strain the djon djon liquid and let it cool OR remove the Maggi cube broth from the heat and let cool. Reserve 1½ cups of broth and set the rest aside.

3. In a rice cooker, add all of the remaining ingredients and stir them together to mix well.

4. Once the rice is cooked, check it. If it appears to be a bit underdone, add in the remaining 1/2 cup of broth and set the rice cooker to the steam function to finish for an additional 5 to 7 minutes.

5. Add the green peas at the very end to keep them green and perky in the rice.

On Recognition Technologies

SOPHIA GIOVANNITTI

In *Mission: Impossible – Rogue Nation* (2015), a government agent gone rogue has to go through a security system that uses gait analysis to confirm the identities of power plant workers, a technology described as *a step beyond facial recognition*. If the stride doesn't match exactly, the worker gets felled by tasers pointed to the chest. The reason for such high security is to safeguard precious information hidden beneath the plant, which, if found, would provide its finder sweeping financial access.

My boyfriend was the first person to tell me about gait analysis. He brought it up as something we should be fearful of for the future, but also as something that's easy to trick, in an analog way, if one is trying to avoid recognition, as opposed to stealing another's identity: put a rock in your shoe. *Isn't that cool*, he said. *These hundred year-old tricks. Like if you rob someone, put a quarter in your mouth—it changes the way you talk.* But you can't annihilate your whole self—surveillance software can scan an entire airport for a hand tattoo, so.

When we go through airports, he asks every time they move to take a photo of your face if it's required. *Pull your mask down,* they'll say. *Can I say no?* he asks. Sometimes you can say no—it's redundant how many times they force you to. *They have you anyway,* he says, *but I'm just not going to make it easy like that; I can't.* It's the same reason he covers his face with a baseball cap during the brief second we pass an overhead camera on the drive into the Rockaways: it's a gesture of refusal, even if total refusal is impossible. I love watching it, with my feet up on the dashboard. So that's another kind of

> **"We will try to use their tools against them. But we will recognize one another, too, with our own technologies."**

recognition technology—hostility to TSA, or the cameras encroaching on the beach.

There's a scene in *Papillon* (1973) where Henri has escaped from prison and needs a boat to remain free and on the run. He is told he can get one at a nearby leper colony. He approaches a guy in the colony who's smoking a cigar, whose face is disfigured from leprosy. The guy tells Henri that they usually kill outsiders. Henri says that makes sense. The guy asks if Henri likes cigars, and Henri says yes. The guy offers Henri the cigar, and Henri takes several deliberate drags, then gives it back. *How did you know I have dry leprosy?* the guy asks. *That it isn't contagious?* Henri answers, *I didn't,* and they laugh and give him the boat.

I think the future will be so much about recognition technology. And it's true, they already have us. There's little we can do, other than rocks in our shoes and quarters in our mouths, and never making it easy. We can make prosthetic fingers to attach to our hands when we shoplift, so that we might claim any incriminating footage is AI-generated: too many digits. We will try to use their tools against them. But we will recognize one another, too, with our own technologies. In a hostile world, there are people who are baseline fearful of others, and will give up all their rights to a hostile state in the name of that fear, and there are people who will try vainly to refuse the photo, or recklessly take the cigar. This is also precious hidden information, and we can find it in each other. I hope, if it comes down to it, I'll take the cigar.

Sunflower

KEEGAN DAKKAR LOMANTO

Weightlifter3

HANNAH BEERMAN

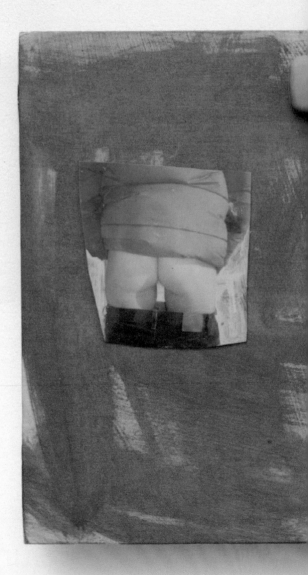

October

THE 10TH MONTH | 31 DAYS

Blood Moon - OCTOBER

Named for the time of year that hunters kill and process animals to eat during winter.

SUNDAY	MONDAY	TUESDAY	WEDNESDAY	THURSDAY	FRIDAY	SATURDAY
		1	**2**	**3**	**4**	**5**
		☼ 6:53 am	☼ 6:54 am	☼ 6:55 am	☼ 6:56 am	☼ 6:57 am
		☼ 6:37 pm	☼ 6:35 pm	☼ 6:33 pm	☼ 6:32 pm	☼ 6:30 pm
		☽ 11:44:02	☽ 11:41:22	☽ 11:38:42	☽ 11:36:02	☽ 11:33:23
		☾ 5:40 am	☾ 6:40 am	☾ 7:40 am	☾ 8:41 am	☾ 9:43 am
		☽ 6:13 pm	☽ 6:32 pm	☽ 6:51 pm	☽ 7:12 pm	☽ 7:37 pm
		♍ Virgo	♎ Libra	♎ Libra	♏ Scorpio	♏ Scorpio
6	**7**	**8**	**9**	**10**	**11**	**12**
☼ 6:58 am	☼ 6:59 am	☼ 7:00 am	☼ 7:01 am	☼ 7:02 am	☼ 7:03 am	☼ 7:04 am
☼ 6:28 pm	☼ 6:27 pm	☼ 6:25 pm	☼ 6:24 pm	☼ 6:22 pm	☼ 6:21 pm	☼ 6:19 pm
☽ 11:30:44	☽ 11:28:05	☽ 11:25:26	☽ 11:22:47	☽ 11:20:09	☽ 11:17:31	☽ 11:14:54
☾ 10:48 am	☾ 11:53 am	☾ 12:55 pm	☾ 1:53 pm	☾ 2:43 pm	☾ 3:25 pm	☾ 12:47 am
☽ 8:07 pm	☽ 8:44 pm	☽ 9:31 pm	☽ 10:28 pm	☽ 11:34 pm		☾ 4:00 pm
♏ Scorpio	♐ Sagittarius	♐ Sagittarius	♑ Capricorn	♑ Capricorn	♑ Capricorn	♒ Aquarius

13 ☼ 7:05 am · ☼ 6:17 pm · ☼ 11:12:17 · ☽ 2:03 am · ☽ 4:30 pm · ♒ Aquarius

14 ☼ 7:06 am · ☼ 6:16 pm · ☼ 11:09:41 · ☽ 3:20 am · ☽ 4:56 pm · ♓ Pisces

15 ☼ 7:07 am · ☼ 6:14 pm · ☼ 11:07:05 · ☽ 4:37 am · ☽ 5:21 pm · ♓ Pisces

16 ☼ 7:08 am · ☼ 6:13 pm · ☼ 11:04:29 · ☽ 5:56 am · ☽ 5:46 pm · ♈ Aries

17 ☼ 7:09 am · ☼ 6:11 pm · ☼ 11:01:54 · ☽ 7:15 am · ☽ 6:13 pm · ♈ Aries

18 ☼ 7:11 am · ☼ 6:10 pm · ☼ 10:59:20 · ☽ 8:37 am · ☽ 6:45 pm · ♉ Taurus

19 ☼ 7:12 am · ☼ 6:08 pm · ☼ 10:56:46 · ☽ 9:59 am · ☽ 7:23 pm · ♉ Taurus

20 ☼ 7:13 am · ☼ 6:07 pm · ☼ 10:54:13 · ☽ 11:17 am · ☽ 8:10 pm · ♊ Gemini

21 ☼ 7:14 am · ☼ 6:06 pm · ☼ 10:51:41 · ☽ 12:27 pm · ☽ 9:06 pm · ♊ Gemini

22 ☼ 7:15 am · ☼ 6:04 pm · ☼ 10:49:09 · ☽ 1:26 pm · ☽ 10:10 pm · ♋ Cancer

23 ☼ 7:16 am · ☼ 6:03 pm · ☼ 10:46:38 · ☽ 2:12 pm · ☽ 11:17 pm · ♋ Cancer

24 ☼ 7:17 am · ☼ 6:01 pm · ☼ 10:44:08 · ☽ 2:48 pm · ♌ Leo

25 ☼ 7:18 am · ☼ 6:00 pm · ☼ 10:41:38 · ☽ 12:25 am · ☽ 3:17 pm · ♌ Leo

26 ☼ 7:20 am · ☼ 5:59 pm · ☼ 10:39:10 · ☽ 1:30 am · ☽ 3:40 pm · ♌ Leo

27 ☼ 7:21 am · ☼ 5:57 pm · ☼ 10:36:42 · ☽ 2:33 am · ☽ 4:01 pm · ♍ Virgo

28 ☼ 7:22 am · ☼ 5:56 pm · ☼ 10:34:15 · ☽ 3:33 am · ☽ 4:20 pm · ♍ Virgo

29 ☼ 7:23 am · ☼ 5:55 pm · ☼ 10:31:50 · ☽ 4:33 am · ☽ 4:38 pm · ♎ Libra

30 ☼ 7:24 am · ☼ 5:54 pm · ☼ 10:29:25 · ☽ 5:32 am · ☽ 4:57 pm · ♎ Libra

31 ☼ 7:25 am · ☼ 5:52 pm · ☼ 10:27:02 · ☽ 6:33 am · ☽ 5:18 pm · ♎ Libra

Key

SUNRISE · SUNSET · DAY LENGTH · MOONRISE · MOONSET

October

Herbal Tips

ECHINACEA

Libra is known for balance, harmony, and justice, which echinacea supports through its immune-boosting properties. Echinacea is commonly used during the fall season when the weather starts to change and the risk of colds and flu increases.

Its ability to stimulate the immune system helps to ward off illness and maintain balance in the body. Additionally, echinacea is said to have a balancing effect on the energy of the throat chakra, which is associated with communication and self-expression.

This aligns with Libra's focus on diplomacy and relationship-building. Overall, echinacea's association with Libra makes it a fitting herb for the month of October in Astro Herbalism. Echinacea is best consumed in tea or tincture form.

Astrology

While the first month of fall is typically known for its creative costumes, elaborate pumpkin carvings, and spooky corn mazes, this year the cosmos are cooking up something extra sweet for Libra season. On October 2, the first Libra Solar Eclipse of the eclipse cycle that began in April 2023 will illuminate the sky. This amplified New Moon is all about embracing the soft life and being gentle with yourself in the process. Luckily, Jupiter—the planet of growth and achievement—will slow down and station retrograde in busy Gemini on October 9, making October a good time to create more space for romance, luxurious experiences, and new partnerships as you will be less focused on attending social gatherings and juggling multiple projects. You'll notice a shift in the chilling air as communicator Mercury slips into secretive Scorpio from October 13 until November 2. During this emotionally charged transit, pay attention to your intuitive instincts and bodily language. The Sun will join Mercury in Scorpio on October 22, and this is an excellent period to sharpen your psychic abilities, improve research skills, and deepen intimate bonds.

Phenology Calendar

In this writer's opinion, October is when New York City is its most perfect—and it's not just because of a previously mentioned affection for candy. It's cozy and spooky and ultimate hoodie weather. Upstate, the autumn foliage is in full force and everything looks like a tasteful ad for apple juice. It's white-tailed deer breeding season; you can see them being especially active (and aggressive) in Pelham Bay Park and Van Cortlandt Park.

Third Act

BILL MCKIBBEN

The ugliest bumper sticker I've ever seen (though there is plenty of competition) was affixed to the back of a Winnebago somewhere down in Arizona. It said: "I'm Spending My Kid's Inheritance."

If you think about it, this is more or less what older Americans have done; we've used up a lot of the world in our decades on it. Boomers got here while the getting was good and we ended up hoarding a lot of the stuff. By some measures, Americans over sixty have 70% of the country's financial resources, compared with only 5% for millennials.

But wealth isn't all we have. We also have a lifetime's worth of skills and connections. We have a generational DNA, a collective memory that includes that period of epic social, cultural, and political transformation at the start of our lives. If you're in your sixties or seventies or eighties, the first act of your life coincided with the emergence of feminist theories in public life, while the civil rights movement was raging and twenty million Americans marched on the first Earth Day.

In 2021, when my collaborators and I launched Third Act, we counted on that transformational spirit still being alive, and our faith has been rewarded. Third Act is building a community of experienced Americans over the age of sixty who are determined to change the world for the better. We are closing in on a hundred thousand volunteers, formed into working groups across the country. Our volunteers have registered huge numbers of voters. They've shut down the country's biggest banks for a day, gathering in rocking chairs at more than ninety locations across the United States to protest the banks' ongoing investment in fossil fuels.

Mostly, Third Act has done all we can to back up the young people who are leading the fight for change. It's right that on questions like climate change youth should be out front—I'll be dead before the very worst of it kicks in, but they will be in mid-stride. The Greta Generation is doing wonderful things, organizing at a more global level than we've ever seen.

For all their energy, idealism, and intelligence, younger people lack the structural power to make the change we need in the time we have. That's where older people can really help, because we have structural power coming out our ears (and also hair). It's not just that we have money—we also vote in huge numbers. We're used to working the system, any system; we're not intimidated by politicians.

One benefit of growing older is that at a certain point you might not take yourself quite as seriously (we march sometimes under a banner that says "Fossils Against Fossil Fuels"). Another benefit of being nearer the exit than the entrance is that some things come into sharper focus, even for aging eyes. "Legacy" is not some abstraction—it's the world you leave behind for the people you love the most. At the moment, my generation is in grave danger of leaving behind a shabbier world than the one we arrived in. We're in grave danger of literally spending our kids' inheritance, but it doesn't need to be that way.

Untitled (Blue and Gold)

DYANI WHITE HAWK

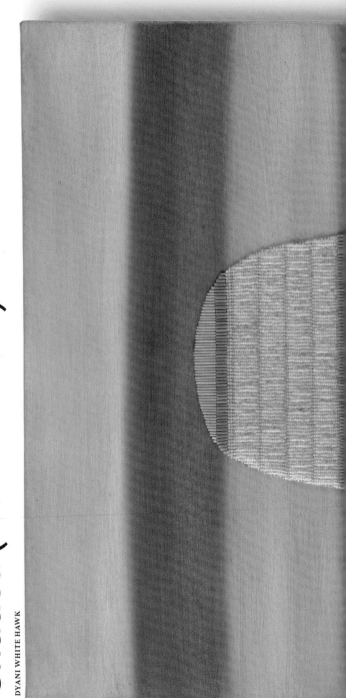

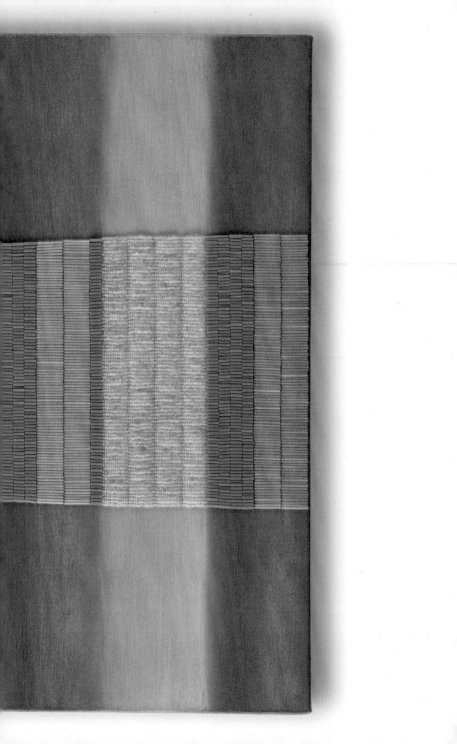

130

November

THE 11TH MONTH | 30 DAYS

NOVEMBER 3RD
Fall back 1 hour.

Key

	SUNRISE	SUNSET	DAY LENGTH	MOONRISE	MOONSET
	☼	☼	☼	☽	☽

SUNDAY	MONDAY	TUESDAY	WEDNESDAY	THURSDAY	FRIDAY	SATURDAY
3	**4**	**5**	**6**	**7**	**1**	**2**
☼ 6:29 am	☼ 6:30 am	☼ 6:31 am	☼ 6:32 am	☼ 6:34 am	☼ 7:27 am	☼ 7:28 am
☼ 4:49 pm	☼ 4:48 pm	☼ 4:47 pm	☼ 4:46 pm	☼ 4:44 pm	☼ 5:51 pm	☼ 5:50 pm
☼ 10:19:59	☼ 10:17:40	☼ 10:15:23	☼ 10:13:08	☼ 10:10:54	☼ 10:24:40	☼ 10:22:19
☽ 8:45 am	☽ 9:49 am	☽ 10:48 am	☽ 11:40 am	☽ 12:24 pm	☽ 7:35 am	☽ 8:40 am
☽ 5:45 pm	☽ 6:29 pm	☽ 7:22 pm	☽ 8:25 pm	☽ 9:34 pm	☽ 5:41 pm	☽ 6:10 pm
♐ Sagittarius	♐ Sagittarius	♐ Sagittarius	♑ Capricorn	♑ Capricorn	♏ Scorpio	♏ Scorpio
				7	**8**	**9**
					☼ 6:35 am	☼ 6:36 am
					☼ 4:43 pm	☼ 4:42 pm
					☼ 10:08:42	☼ 10:06:31
					☽ 1:00 pm	☽ 1:30 pm
					☽ 10:47 pm	
					≈ Aquarius	≈ Aquarius

	10	11	12	13	14	15	16
☼	6:37 am	6:38 am	6:39 am	6:41 am	6:42 am	6:43 am	6:44 am
☼	4:41 pm	4:41 pm	4:40 pm	4:39 pm	4:38 pm	4:37 pm	4:36 pm
☼	10:04:22	10:02:15	10:00:09	9:58:06	9:56:05	9:54:05	9:52:08
☾	12:01 am	1:15 am	2:30 am	3:46 am	5:05 am	6:26 am	7:48 am
☾	1:56 pm	2:21 pm	2:45 pm	3:10 pm	3:39 pm	4:13 pm	4:56 pm
	♓ Pisces	♓ Pisces	♈ Aries	♈ Aries	♉ Taurus	♉ Taurus	♊ Gemini

	17	18	19	20	21	22	23
☼	6:45 am	6:46 am	6:48 am	6:49 am	6:50 am	6:51 am	6:52 am
☼	4:36 pm	4:35 pm	4:34 pm	4:33 pm	4:33 pm	4:32 pm	4:32 pm
☼	9:50:13	9:48:20	9:46:30	9:44:42	9:42:57	9:41:14	9:39:34
☾	9:04 am	10:10 am	11:04 am	11:45 am	12:17 pm	12:43 pm	1:05 pm
☾	5:49 pm	6:52 pm	8:00 pm	9:10 pm	10:18 pm	11:22 pm	
	♊ Gemini	♋ Cancer	♋ Cancer	♋ Cancer	♌ Leo	♌ Leo	♍ Virgo

	24	25	26	27	28	29	30
☼	6:53 am	6:54 am	6:55 am	6:57 am	6:58 am	6:59 am	7:00 am
☼	4:31 pm	4:31 pm	4:30 pm	4:30 pm	4:30 pm	4:29 pm	4:29 pm
☼	9:37:56	9:36:21	9:34:50	9:33:21	9:31:55	9:30:32	9:29:12
☾	12:24 am	1:24 am	2:23 am	3:24 am	4:25 am	5:29 am	6:34 am
☾	1:25 pm	1:43 pm	2:02 pm	2:22 pm	2:45 pm	3:12 pm	3:45 pm
	♍ Virgo	♎ Libra	♎ Libra	♎ Libra	♏ Scorpio	♏ Scorpio	♐ Sagittarius

Beaver Moon - NOVEMBER

Named for the beavers who get very busy preparing for the colder months.

November

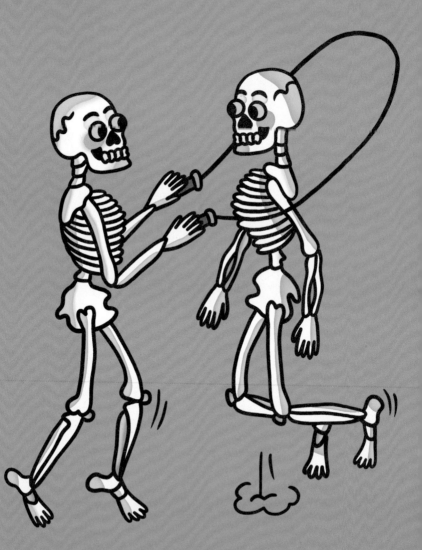

Astrology

November's crisp astrological skies forecast opportunities to host intimate gatherings with close friends, finalize end-of-the-year travel plans, and express gratitude for the year's hard work and harvest. While Scorpio season is typically known for its intensity and moodiness, Mercury's entrance into joyful Sagittarius from November 2 until November 25 makes it hard to stay stuck in a rut this month. Instead of obsessing over what and who you can't change during the Scorpio New Moon on November 1, the Sagittarian-like vibes this November encourage you to try an optimistic approach and choose to find the good in tough situations. While the end of the year is great for reflection, don't be afraid to branch out and try something new if you feel inspired to create or take a calculated risk on November 3, when motivational Mars moves into brave-hearted Leo. Others may not understand your motives or concept at first, but they'll be more inclined to support your efforts once Venus enters commitment-oriented Capricorn on November 11 and Saturn—the planet of public achievement—ends its retrograde in restless Pisces on November 15.

Herbal Tips

ASHWAGANDHA

Ashwagandha is highly valued in Ayurveda for its adaptogenic properties, which help the body to cope with physical and emotional stress. In Astro Herbalism, Ashwagandha is associated with the energy of the sign of Scorpio, which is dominant during November. Scorpio is a sign that is associated with intensity and transformation, and Ashwagandha is believed to help people navigate through the transformative energies of life. This herb helps to increase levels of the hormone cortisol, which helps the body to cope with stress and anxiety. It is also a powerful antioxidant that helps to protect the body from oxidative stress, which can lead to cellular damage and inflammation. It is also used as a tonic for the immune system, helping to strengthen the body's defenses against infection and disease. Ashwagandha can help us to stay grounded and centered, and to navigate through the potent energies of this transformative time of year. Make homemade ashwagandha gummies using organic gelatin, maple syrup, and organic ashwagandha for a tasty, daily health treat.

Phenology Calendar

Daylight saving in November means it's officially time to fully embrace your cozy side. Time itself wants you to sleep in. You should bring your plants, and yourself, inside, because it is time for the first frost.

Edenic Time

JESSIE KINDIG

Edenic time is outside of time, which means it is all times at once in the way that white contains all colors. In Edenic time, everything is still and endless; everything is quick and moving. The world is thick with ghosts, chock-full of the people and insects and plants and trees that once lived or will someday live. It is very hard to find a place to sit. Herds of bison roam the Great Plains, running beside Mesozoic whale-like creatures that swim through the ghost-ocean from before the plains were dry. The skies of Edenic time are thick with passenger pigeons and charged with the snap of every bat eating every mosquito that ever was. The songs of wolf packs, unkilled, ring the mountains like a necklace.

Edenic time lets you meet your family. Bipedal monkeys play catch with human children. The passenger pigeon finally meets its distant cousin, the mourning dove, and further distant cousin, the pterodactyl. Trees root into soil composted from the pinecone children their grand-trees will someday bear. Prokaryotic microbes jumble together with coronaviruses and are gathered up by water bears like Easter-basket jellybeans.

horsetail has to say to a horse are simply understood by all. In Edenic time, there is no mediation, only the immediacy of experience. Another nice thing about Edenic time is that misunderstandings are impossible and there is no need for small talk.

No one cares about the dialectic in Edenic time, which is to say that everyone cares about it, because caring and not caring are the same thing. There is so much going on in one square foot of the world in Edenic time that you could stand there forever watching it all. When you do, you will become a tree. As you become a tree and your feet-paws-hooves-claws push into the earth, you will feel the electric bolt of roots pushing against the earth's mycelial wrapping, far underground. Soon you will sense every part of everywhere in Edenic time, from simply standing still and watching your one square foot.

In Edenic time, there are no worries about language, because ghosts don't care too much for verbs. One of the joys of Edenic time is that you know everything you will ever know and learn each thing you will come to know simultaneously. Language is superfluous in this endeavor—what the snakes whisper to the women, and how the Late Permian turtles of Turtle Island move underfoot, and what a

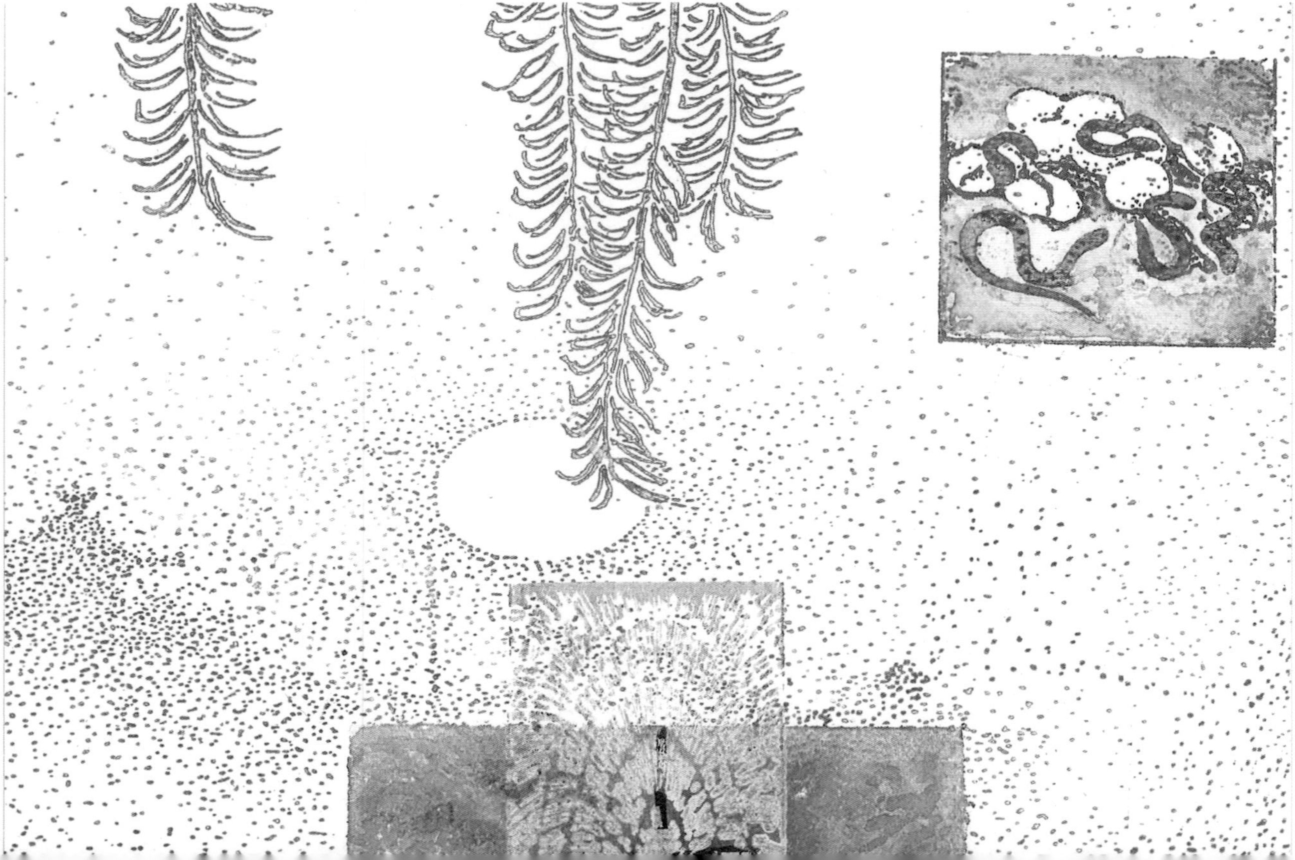

The Shadow of Night Makes Way for Morning Light

CHRIS LLOYD

Reflections On the Modern Dialectics of Preservation and Erasure

JUMANA MANNA

Archives purportedly intend to preserve a record of cultural forms at risk of disappearance. They are also governed by a fateful paradox: archival practices' hierarchies and biases are derived from historical processes at the root of the erasure of those very forms.

These polarities that frame relations of preservation and decay are a defining characteristic of colonialism, and settler-colonialism in particular, because the settler's mission is centered on naturalizing his claim to a territory. This form of governance involves managing all of what lives and dies on, beneath, and above the land: a negotiation and shifting definition of settler life, through the genocidal erasure of native presence. In settler-colonies, nationalized landscapes are created by a dominant group imposing its well-being over the well-being of a subjugated group; the former completely or partially replaces the landscape symbols, life forms, and structures of the latter. Sustaining the settler-

life-symbols at times includes an appropriation of native cultures by treating them as landscape. This wholesale appropriation of the territory (the land and the culture of the people on the land) differentiates it from the more explicit extractivist/exploitative strategies of classical colonialism.

Across these differing histories, preserving and archiving institutions have functioned as scaffolding to the colonial state, upholding the supremacy

> "Across these differing histories, preserving and archiving institutions have functioned as scaffolding to the colonial state, upholding the supremacy of its life symbols and legitimacy of its reason."

of its life symbols and legitimacy of its reason.

Consider the history of museums, which comes into being with and through the nation-state. Situated at the nexus of colonial knowledge-power, museums store, care for, and display objects—ethnographic, archaeological, or otherwise—that have been uprooted through colonial plunder. They house objects that have been pulled out of their environments and temporalities, displaced into the sterile, frozen time of storage and display rooms.

The discipline of archaeology developed in parallel to the rise of museums and is a central example of preserving and archiving. While studying the material culture of earlier epochs is often illuminating, the field of archaeology as a formalized discipline has been tainted by its drive to power. Archaeological tools and findings are used and misused to assert national narratives that exist to claim land or territory through the erasure and exclusion of other groups that do not fit the fabrications of the nation-state. Similarly, botanists and botanical gardens that studied morphologies and behaviors of plants were part of systems and institutional bodies that assisted the transfer of plants from colonial regions all over the world to Europe. This discipline, which was also dedicated to the preservation and cultivation of diverse species, laid the foundation for colonial power dynamics that extracted a self-multiplying resource—seeds—to benefit the economic dominance of the Global North. Nature conservation emerged entangled with cultural centers that perpetuate naturalization of racial relations and power in other forms.

Throughout capitalist modernity, which is colonial in past and present, every act of preservation has entailed an erasure of sorts, not because that's the destiny of any preservation effort, but because modernity operates through the splitting of life-worlds in two. Certain groups of people are made masters and others slaves; certain life forms, documents, or practices get marked for care, while others get discarded or left to rot. Objects that have higher exchange value are continuously prioritized over other objects and over social lives.

As much as these relations have defined the dialectic of preservation and erasure throughout modernity, they have never wholly defined or sealed life and landscape. From revolts to everyday cultural practices and unannounced ways of remaining present, communities have resisted erasure and cultural dissolution. Looking to, learning from, and prioritizing these resistance practices is essential to breaking

"While studying the material culture of earlier epochs is often illuminating, the field of archaeology as a formalized discipline has been tainted by its drive to power."

out of the inheritances of slavery and colonialism in all their contemporary forms, away from perpetuated logics of extinction and towards forms of preservation as everyday cultures of care. Ecologies must be rebuilt and re-symbolized so they are geared towards mutuality and affirmation, rather than segregation and exclusion. In my

"Ecologies must be rebuilt and re-symbolized so they are geared towards mutuality and affirmation, rather than segregation and exclusion."

films, I have looked at how small farmers exemplify this everyday culture of living care by planting, exchanging, and eating heirloom varieties, thereby preserving biodiversity. They tend to these varieties in situ, allowing the seeds to adapt to their microsoils and shifting climates. Despite enduring colonial violence, these rural communities operate as custodians of the land, which gives them sustenance and life in turn. Within its life cycle, the seed dies in order to be re-born again; forests may be burned in controlled burning practices to allow for new life to emerge on the soil. Learning from biological processes gives tools of steadfastness in a life of ruination. This steadfastness is not a complacency or a welcoming of that violence, but rather a resistance to the ongoing structures of oppression in the aftermath of violence. The violence of the event is accepted as part of life, because life and liveliness must continue amidst it. Death and decay get redefined by the oppressed as a part of life and its regeneration, not only in the organic realm, but in the infrastructural and psychological as well.

As preservation is part of the maintenance of life, the question is not whether to preserve, but who gets to decide what lives on and how. Imagining how an ecology of preservation and decay can embody social justice and self-determination of the implicated populations, human and otherwise, is the key towards planetary emancipation.

December

THE 12TH MONTH | 31 DAYS

Cold Moon - DECEMBER
Named for the start of winter.

SUNDAY	MONDAY	TUESDAY	WEDNESDAY	THURSDAY	FRIDAY	SATURDAY
1	**2**	**3**	**4**	**5**	**6**	**7**
☿ 7:01 am	☿ 7:02 am	☿ 7:03 am	☿ 7:04 am	☿ 7:05 am	☿ 7:06 am	☿ 7:06 am
☿ 4:29 pm	☿ 4:28 pm	☿ 4:28 pm	☿ 4:28 pm	☿ 4:28 pm	☿ 4:28 pm	☿ 4:28 pm
☿☿ 9:27:56	☿☿ 9:26:43	☿☿ 9:25:33	☿☿ 9:24:27	☿☿ 9:23:24	☿☿ 9:22:25	☿☿ 9:21:30
☽ 7:40 am	☽ 8:41 am	☽ 9:37 am	☽ 10:23 am	☽ 11:01 am	☽ 11:33 am	☽ 11:59 am
☽ 4:26 pm	☽ 5:17 pm	☽ 6:18 pm	☽ 7:26 pm	☽ 8:38 pm	☽ 9:51 pm	☽ 11:03 pm
♓ Pisces	♐ Sagittarius	♑ Capricorn	♑ Capricorn	≈ Aquarius	≈ Aquarius	♓ Pisces
8	**9**	**10**	**11**	**12**	**13**	**14**
☿ 7:07 am	☿ 7:08 am	☿ 7:09 am	☿ 7:10 am	☿ 7:11 am	☿ 7:11 am	☿ 7:12 am
☿ 4:28 pm	☿ 4:28 pm	☿ 4:28 pm	☿ 4:28 pm	☿ 4:28 pm	☿ 4:29 pm	☿ 4:29 pm
☿☿ 9:20:38	☿☿ 9:19:50	☿☿ 9:19:05	☿☿ 9:18:25	☿☿ 9:17:48	☿☿ 9:17:15	☿☿ 9:16:47
☽ 12:24 pm	☽ 12:15 pm	☽ 1:28 am	☽ 2:43 am	☽ 4:00 am	☽ 5:20 am	☽ 6:38 am
☽ —	☽ 12:47 pm	☽ 1:10 pm	☽ 1:36 pm	☽ 2:07 pm	☽ 2:45 pm	☽ 3:33 pm
♓ Pisces	♓ Pisces	♈ Aries	♈ Aries	♉ Taurus	♉ Taurus	♊ Gemini

15
☉ 7:13 am
☉ 4:29 pm
☀ 9:16:22
☽ 7:49 am
☾ 4:31 pm
♊ Gemini

16
☉ 7:13 am
☉ 4:29 pm
☀ 9:16:01
☽ 8:49 am
☾ 5:38 pm
♋ Cancer

17
☉ 7:14 am
☉ 4:30 pm
☀ 9:15:44
☽ 9:37 am
☾ 6:49 pm
♋ Cancer

18
☉ 7:15 am
☉ 4:30 pm
☀ 9:15:31
☽ 10:14 am
☾ 8:00 pm
♌ Leo

19
☉ 7:15 am
☉ 4:31 pm
☀ 9:15:22
☽ 10:43 am
☾ 9:07 pm
♌ Leo

20
☉ 7:16 am
☉ 4:31 pm
☀ 9:15:17
☽ 11:07 am
☾ 10:11 pm
♍ Virgo

21
☉ 7:16 am
☉ 4:32 pm
☀ 9:15:16
☽ 11:28 am
☾ 11:13 pm
♍ Virgo

22
☉ 7:17 am
☉ 4:32 pm
☀ 9:15:20
☽ 11:47 am
♍ Virgo

23
☉ 7:17 am
☉ 4:33 pm
☀ 9:15:27
☽ 12:05 pm
☾ 12:13 am
♎ Libra

24
☉ 7:18 am
☉ 4:33 pm
☀ 9:15:39
☽ 12:25 pm
☾ 1:12 am
♎ Libra

25
☉ 7:18 am
☉ 4:34 pm
☀ 9:15:54
☽ 12:46 pm
☾ 2:13 am
♏ Scorpio

26
☉ 7:18 am
☉ 4:35 pm
☀ 9:16:14
☽ 1:12 pm
☾ 3:16 am
♏ Scorpio

27
☉ 7:19 am
☉ 4:35 pm
☀ 9:16:37
☽ 1:42 pm
☾ 4:21 am
♏ Scorpio

28
☉ 7:19 am
☉ 4:36 pm
☀ 9:17:05
☽ 2:20 pm
☾ 5:26 am
♐ Sagittarius

29
☉ 7:19 am
☉ 4:37 pm
☀ 9:17:36
☽ 3:08 pm
☾ 6:30 am
♐ Sagittarius

30
☉ 7:19 am
☉ 4:38 pm
☀ 9:18:12
☽ 4:07 pm
☾ 7:29 am
♑ Capricorn

31
☉ 7:19 am
☉ 4:38 pm
☀ 9:18:51
☽ 5:14 pm
☾ 8:19 am
♑ Capricorn

Key

SUNRISE	☉
SUNSET	☉
DAY LENGTH	☀
MOONRISE	☽
MOONSET	☾

December

Astrology

As the year draws to a close and the stars align to promote the extraordinary magic of the Sagittarius New Moon peaking on December 1, allow your heart and mind to be filled with appreciation for all that is and hope for all that will be. Prepare yourself for deeper and more honest conversations in the coming weeks, as messenger Mercury continues its final retrograde of the year in philosophical Sagittarius

from December 1 until December 15. While it's important to tap into the generous spirit of Sagittarius season, keep an eye out for insecurity issues that may dampen your self-confidence around December 6, when motivational Mars stations retrograde in Leo. Although Leo is known as a sign of bravery and courage, Mars's retrograde position may cause you to doubt your uniqueness. Luckily, any self-sabotaging thinking

blocking your blessings will rise to the surface during the enlightening Gemini Full Moon on December 15. Use this empowering lunation to affirm your worth and release comparison fears. If looking for a favorable time to set intentions for the new year, try the Capricorn New Moon on December 30. This energy is excellent for getting a head start on your 2025 vision!

Phenology Calendar

December: one of the most embarrassing times of year to be a sentimental New Yorker easily swayed by capitalist pantomimes of holiday cheer. Chestnuts are roasting, sleigh bells are ringing. Tourists with rosy cheeks migrate through Times Square and Rockefeller Center, while whales migrate from Alaska through Rockaway Beach. You can see upwards of 20,000 of both.

Herbal Tips

REISHI MUSHROOM

Reishi mushrooms are also known as the "mushroom of immortality" and are a popular ingredient in traditional Chinese medicine. Medicinal mushrooms like reishi should always be consumed when heated or in tincture form to ensure that all of the nutrients and compounds have been effectively extracted. Here's a simple recipe for a yummy reishi latte:

Ingredients

- · 1 cup of organic raw milk or milk alternative (almond, cashew, coconut, etc.)
- · 1 teaspoon of reishi mushroom powder
- · 1 teaspoon of honey or maple syrup (optional)
- · 1 teaspoon of vanilla extract (optional)

Instructions

1. Heat the milk in a small pot over medium heat. Do not boil the milk.

2. Add the reishi mushroom powder and whisk continuously until the powder dissolves completely.

3. Add the optional sweetener and vanilla extract and whisk again until everything is well combined.

4. Remove the pot from the heat and pour the latte into a mug.

5. Enjoy your delicious reishi latte that can boost the immune system, reduce inflammation, help with stress and anxiety, and improve sleep quality.

6. Overall, a reishi latte is a tasty and simple way to add more medicinal mushrooms to your diet and reap their many health benefits.

The Mall

PHILIP POON

It's become known as "the mall." If you're in the NYC art, fashion, or design world, it's likely that you're familiar with it. It's where the cool kids are. Of course Jerry Saltz has been there.

It was built in 2004 right underneath Manhattan Bridge, on land that the city owns. The deafening sounds and vibrations of the subways crossing the bridge overhead made the site undesirable, but the building nevertheless served as an important place for Chinese immigrants to buy basic necessities. The building was separated into two halves bifurcated by a wide alleyway; one half was a shopping mall that sold clothing, beauty products, and Chinese medicine, while the other half housed a supermarket and restaurant.

Everything sold there was affordable, cheap, because the mall was for the working class population in the area. It was Chinese through and through—Chinese people, Chinese products, Chinese signage.

The architecture was also Chinese, or Chinese-American. There were no overhanging roofs, orientalized patterns, or dragons (those stylistic tropes are often just cartoonish references to a historicized China anyway). On the contrary, the building was authentically Chinese in its modesty, detailing, and layout. The facades were an economical brick and at the entrances red and blue brick was used to create simple geometric patterns. The interior finishes were generic, but somehow generic in a Chinese way: acoustic tile ceilings and polished gray stone flooring, but with simple patterning along some edges. Perhaps the most recognizably Chinese-American aspect of the interior was the shiny stainless steel handrails that are so readily associated with Chinese homes in Flushing and Sunset Park. The simple layout of the spaces further lent to the authentic modesty of the building.

Things in the mall started to change in 2016, when a white guy opened a record store on the second floor, the kind of record store where customers are serious about the sound quality of vinyl. In addition to experimental music records, there were also art books, the kind of art books with purple CGI mannequin heads in them. The store had a faux Asian-sounding name and a tongue-in-cheek neon sign written in Chinese characters. Gift cards were sold in Chinese red envelopes, the kind that are exchanged during Lunar New Year between parents and their children.

The kind that my parents give to me.

Soon enough, other art, fashion, and high culture boutiques moved into the second floor spaces. Some followed suit and also had their signage written in Chinese characters. Today, the entire second floor is occupied by art galleries, fashion boutiques, and designer furniture stores. There have been countless write-ups in *Vogue*, *The New York Times*, *Artforum*, and similar publications.

The language these publications use to describe the mall and its Chinese-ness is the same. In the beginning, the galleries and boutiques were "discrete" and "hidden," "secrets" that were "nestled" in an anonymous Chinatown space. References to the working class Chinese tenants on the first floor of the mall were explicitly classist, but only obliquely racial, often couched in descriptors like "peculiar," "eerie," "disorienting," and "otherworldly."

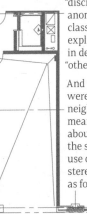

And yet, the idea that these new tenants were well-integrated with their Chinese neighbors was a common thread. I mean, what are they expected to believe about themselves? That they were "gentrifying" the space? That their presence in the mall and use of its aesthetics actively relied on racist stereotypes of working class Chinese immigrants as foreign, strange, and less than? What is "cultural appropriation" anyway? It is human nature to believe oneself to be good. I can understand how a writer in *Vogue* isn't going to address the uncomfortable racial dynamics of the space, and their own complicity as a member of the culture class, in a 500-word write-up.

Particularly complex is the place of Asian-Americans, specifically culture-class Asian-Americans, in the mall. The writer who described the Chinese setting of the mall as an "installation-like environment" for high fashion is herself Asian. Influential Asian-American celebrities shop at the fashion boutiques, and the galleries sometimes show works by Asian-American artists. A well known Asian-American writer wrote enthusiastically about the record store that started it all, the record store with the fake Chinese sign and gift cards in red envelopes.

I also saw on Instagram that one of the second floor galleries follows a girl I met on Tinder, an art-adjacent white girl.

My dad is the architect who built the mall. When I asked him about his thought process in designing the mall, I was surprised by how sincere he was. The different colored brick patterns at the entrances were "gates" that welcomed people from all sides of the building. Two lights at the top of each gate served as beacons. The alleyway that separated the two halves was a strategy to avoid interfering with the structural integrity of the bridge piers, while also providing a public outdoors space.

He wasn't trying to make something weird, or foreign, or strange. He was trying to design the best building he could. Embedded in his sincerity is the idea that architecture is a force for good.

I asked my dad whether it would be accurate to describe the mall as "working class" when it was first built, and he said yes. That part of Chinatown had a high concentration of Fujianese immigrants at that time; it was not a fancy part of Chinatown. He said that Fujianese immigrants were known as "boat people" because of an incident in 1993 when a ship carrying undocumented Chinese immigrants ran aground by the Rockaways in Queens. "Google it," he said.

I did, and found a front page article in the New York Times that described a horrific journey that ended with ten people drowning and hundreds arrested by immigration authorities. The language used to describe these people was different in 1993; the writer referred to them as "illegal Chinese aliens." Further research uncovered videos and photos of the tragic event: hundreds of Chinese people shivering on the beach before being arrested.

Boat people. So the opposite of *Crazy Rich Asians*. The opposite of culture class.

This is the historical and present-day context in which the mall exists. The building embodies the complexities and contradictions of contemporary culture today in New York City, with all the simultaneously explicit and unspoken realities about race and class. Are Asian-Americans "people of color?" The vintage Comme des Garcons sweater sold on the second floor is a great deal. I mean, I couldn't read the fake Chinese signage of the record store anyway. But why does Jerry Saltz' anti-Trump liberalism bother me so much?

Mehmana/Guests

HANGAMA AMIRI

Community Gardens of New York

Below are listed just a few of the many community gardens in New York State. For complete maps and lists visit:

For New York City community gardens

For New York State community gardens

Albany County

Livingston Avenue Community Garden

419 Livingston Avenue
Albany, NY

Edward Street Community Garden

7 Edward Street
Cohoes, NY

Rensselaer Family Garden

1510 5th Street
Rensselaer, NY

Broome County

Gregory Lane Community Garden

9 Gregory Lane
Binghamton, NY

Liberty Street Community Garden

79 Liberty Street
Binghamton, NY

Bronx County

Belmont Little Farmers

2485 Belmont Avenue
Bronx, NY

Dred Scott Bird Sanctuary Garden

1304 Grant Avenue
Bronx, NY

Chautauqua County

Washington Street Community Garden

Washington Street
Jamestown, NY

Allen Street Community Garden

Allen Street
Jamestown, NY

Cayuga County

Case Mansion Community Garden

180 South Street
Auburn, NY

St. Francis Park

25 Underwood Street
Auburn, NY

Chemung County

Tanglewoods Nature Rangers

215 Partridge Street
Elmira, NY

Clinton County

Plattsburgh Community Garden

4817 South Catherine Street
Plattsburgh, NY

Columbia County

Crellin Park Community Garden

Crellin Park
Chatham, NY

Salaam BIPOC Community Garden

20 School Teacher Road
Hudson, New York

Cortland County

Youth Community Garden

3 South Avenue
Cortland, NY

Delaware County

Farm Catskills

87 Sal Bren Road
Delhi, NY

Dutchess County

Red Hook Community Garden

7282-7296 South Broadway
Red Hook, NY

Fall Kill Partnership Garden

29 North Hamilton Street
Poughkeepsie, NY

Erie County

Fruitbelt Coalition

37 Mulberry Street
Buffalo, NY

Lugar Hermoso de Pedro Community Garden

Corner of Hudson Street &
West Avenue
Buffalo, NY

Essex County

Schroon Lake Community Garden

Main Street
Schroon Lake, NY

Florence Hathaway Park Community Garden

Florence Hathaway Park
Essex Road
Willsboro, NY

Franklin County

Tupper Lake Community Garden

120 Demars Boulevard
Tupper Lake, NY

Common Ground Garden

254 Old Lake Colby Road
Saranac Lake, NY

Bloomingdale Elementary School Garden

79 Canaras Avenue
Saranac Lake, NY

Fulton County

Fremont Neighborhood Garden

Fremont Street & Forest
Street
Gloversville, NY

Jefferson County

Zenda Community Garden

38973 Zenda Farm Road
Clayton, NY

Kings County

Bedford Stuyvesant Community Garden (Lola Bryant Community Garden)

95 Malcolm X Boulevard
Brooklyn, NY

El Puente: Espiritu Tierra Community Garden - Earth Spirit

203-207 South 2nd Street
Brooklyn, NY

Monroe County

In the City Off the Grid

55 Plover Street
Rochester, NY

Neighbors Together

Garson Street &
Chamberlain Street
Rochester, NY

Nassau County

Seed to Table Community Garden

171 Lakeview Avenue
Freeport, NY

Sherman Brown Community Garden

Riverside Boulevard & East
Pine Street
Long Beach, NY

New York County

133rd Swing Street Garden

155 West 133rd Street

Campos Community Garden

640-644 East 12th Street

Niagara County

Ontario Street Community Garden

Ontario Street & Hawley Street
Lockport, NY

Highland Community Vegetable Garden

1800 Beech Avenue
Niagara Falls, NY

Oneida County

Somali Bantu Community Gardens & Education Project

Vega/Martinez Community Center
1736 Armory Drive
Utica, NY

Housing Visions' Garden

40 Grant Street
Utica, NY

Ontario County

Canandaigua Churches in Action

5188 Bristol Road
Canandaigua, NY

Naples, NY Community Gardens

North End of Main Street
Naples, NY

Onondaga County

NOPL Cicero Library Farm

8699 Knowledge Lane
Cicero, NY

Rahma Clinic Edible Forest Snack Garden

3100 South Salina Street
Syracuse, NY

Otsego County

City of Oneonta Community Gardens

Wilcox Avenue
Oneonta, NY

Orange County

Newburgh Armory Community Garden

321-355 South William Street
Newburgh, NY

Port Jervis Community Garden

Intersection of North Street & Main Street
Port Jervis, NY

Orleans County

Community Action Garden

409 East State Street
Albion, NY

Oswego County

Oswego Community Garden

70 East Schuyler Street
Oswego, NY

Putnam County

Tilly Foster Community Garden

Prospect Hill Road, across from Tilly Farm Entrance
Brewster, NY

Queens County

Curtis "50 Cent" Jackson Community Garden

117-09 165th Street
Queens, NY

Rockaway Roots Urban Farm

308 Beach 58th Street
Queens, NY

Rensselaer County

The Preserve Community Garden

76 Wynantskill Way
Troy, NY

Vanderhyden & Fifth Community Garden

2541 5th Avenue
Troy, NY

Richmond County

Roots of Peace Community Garden

390 Targee Street
Staten Island, NY

Westervelt Community & Family Garden

143 Westervelt Avenue
Staten Island, NY

Rockland County

Haverstraw Community Garden

50 Broad Street
Haverstraw, NY

Nyack Community Garden

80 Depew Road
Nyack, NY

Saint Lawrence County

Ogdensburg Community Garden

Route 68 Arterial Highway
Ogdensburg, NY

Saratoga County

Saratoga Springs Community Garden

81 Lincoln Avenue
Saratoga Springs, NY

Halfmoon Heights Community Garden

24 Saratoga Drive
Halfmoon, NY

Schenectady County

Steinmetz Park Community Garden

2151 Lenox Road
Schenectady, NY

Craig & Wyllie Community Garden

981 Craig Street
Schenectady, NY

Suffolk County

YES Community Garden

555 Clayton Avenue
Central Islip, NY

Garden of Feedin'

233 North Country Road
Mt. Sinai, NY

Tompkins County

Project Growing Hope Ithaca Community Garden

Route 13 at Third Street
Ithaca, NY

The Jane Minor BIPOC Community Medicine Garden

40 Burns Road
Brooktondale, NY 14817

Ulster County

YMCA Children and Community Garden

Susan Street
Kingston, NY

New Paltz Gardens for Nutrition

51 Huguenot Street
New Paltz, NY

Wayne County

Newark Rotary Club/ Catholic Family Center of Wayne County

439 West Maple Ave
Newark, NY

Warren County

Sagamore Street Playground

Corner of Sagamore Street &
Hunter Street
Glens Falls, NY

Village Green Community Garden

South Delaware Avenue
Glens Falls, NY

Washington County

Fort Edward Community Garden

Corner of Canal Street &
East Street
Fort Edward, NY

Cambridge Community Garden

Washington Street
Cambridge, NY

Westchester County

Marsh Sanctuary Community Garden/ Intergenerate

114 South Bedford Road
Mt. Kisco, NY

Peekskill Community Garden

Route 6
Peekskill, NY

Community Fridges

A community fridge is a refrigerator stocked with free food. They are located in public spaces and enable food to be shared among members of a neighborhood. Some have attached pantries for non-perishable foods. Food can be added or taken by anyone.

International

NYC

153

Mutual Aid Groups of NY

Below are listed just a few of the many mutual aid groups in New York State. For more complete maps and lists visit:

Bronx

The Pillars

The PILLARS is a holistic recovery community outreach and resource center. Their comprehensive network of partnerships ensures all who are in recovery and those loving someone in active addiction can receive the support they need.

PILLARSNYC.ORG

NYC Common Pantry

NYC Common Pantry is working toward reducing hunger and food insecurities through many programs that establish long term sustainability. They distribute food that is fresh and balanced for people in need.

NYCOMMONPANTRY.ORG

Brooklyn

Environmental Action Lab

Environmental Action Lab is an environmental nonprofit that wants to help bring food justice to NYC. They offer a free urban farming mentorship program aimed towards high school students.

ENVIROACTIONLAB.COM

Bushwick Ayuda Mutua

Bushwick Ayuda Mutua is a collective group of Bushwick residents, long-term residents, and recent arrivals, rooted in the mission of creating a local network for neighbors to support neighbors.

BUSHWICKAYUDAMUTUA.COM

Manhattan

Canal Cafeteria

Canal Cafeteria is a mutual aid group aimed at creating a more equitable food landscape by distributing fresh groceries to working class families and individuals in the Lower East Side of Manhattan.

CANALCAFETERIA.COM

Clio

Formerly known as Washington Heights SeniorLink, Clio provides phone/mail social support, needs assessments, informational resources, and care packages to older adults in the Washington Heights area.

CLIOCONNECT.ORG

Queens

Chhaya CDC

Chhaya CDC was founded in 2000 to advocate for the housing needs of New York City's South Asian community. Their mission is to work with New Yorkers of South Asian origin to advocate for and build economically stable, sustainable, and thriving communities.

CHHAYACDC.ORG

South East Queens United Professionals Front

WSEQUPF invests in the well-being of neighbors and their community by pooling their resources and time to promote locally-sourced goods and services, strengthen social cohesion, and power equitable ventures that enrich the quality of life in Southeast Queens.

FACEBOOK.COM/ GROUPS/305614520239799/ ABOUT

Rockaway Mutual Aid and Support Network

This group is intended to be a space to provide resources, assistance, and connections between members of our community who may be suffering or unable to provide for their basic needs in the midst of the COVID-19 epidemic. The values of solidarity, mutual care, and direct action underlie our actions as a group.

Staten Island

The Moving Support Project

The Moving Support Project helps formerly unhoused people secure furniture to make their space into a real home. The furniture they secure can be anything from couches and beds to wall art. They search for free or cheap furniture online and coordinate with people who are willing to donate their items.

OPENCOLLECTIVE.COM/THEMOV-INGSUPPORTPROJECT

New York City Wide

The Bowery Mission

The Bowery Mission serves homeless and hungry New Yorkers by providing services that meet their immediate needs and transform their lives from poverty and hopelessness to hope.

BOWERY.ORG

Domestic Workers United

Advocating for fair labor standards for nannies, house cleaners, and elder caregivers in NYC.

DWUNEWYORK@GMAIL.COM

Apothecaries / Botanicas / Wellness Centers *From the Database of Black healers and herbalists*

Full database

The Herbal Scoop
Narrowsburg, NY
@the.herbal.scoop
THEHERBALSCOOP.COM

Sacred Vibes Apothecary
Brooklyn, NY
@sacredvibesapothecary
SACREDVIBESHEALING.COM

HealHaus
Brooklyn, NY
@healhaus
HEALHAUS.COM

Rootwork Herbals
Ithaca, NY
@rootworkherbals
ROOTWORKHERBALS.COM

MINKA brooklyn
Brooklyn, NY
@minkabrooklyn
MINKABROOKLYN.COM

10th Floor Studio is the collective work of Jerome Tavé and Kyle Lawson. The two met in 2008 while studying at Savannah College of Art & Design. They combined their personal studio practices in early 2018. Long stints of material experimentation, and cross-species exploration have brought fungi to the center of their work. In a time where climate action cannot be ignored, they hope to use their studio practice to contribute to the shift away from anthropocentric narratives.

adrienne maree brown grows healing ideas in public through her multi-genre writing, her music and her podcasts. Informed by 25 years of movement facilitation, somatics, Octavia E Butler scholarship and her work as a doula, adrienne has nurtured Emergent Strategy, Pleasure Activism, Radical Imagination and Transformative Justice as ideas and practices for transformation. She is the author/editor of several published texts, cogenerator of a tarot deck and a developing musical ritual.

Alexis Pauline Gumbs is a queer Black feminist scholar and writer and an aspirational cousin to all life. Alexis is the author of several books, most recently Undrowned: Black Feminist Lessons from Marine Mammals. She lives in Durham, NC.

Alfredo Jaar is an artist, architect and filmmaker who lives in New York.

Amaryllis R. Flowers is a Queer Puerto Rican American artist living and working in Cairo, NY. Raised between multiple cities and rural communities across America in a constantly shifting landscape, her practice explores themes of hybridity, mythology and sexuality. She was the inaugural AIR for the 2023 Pocantico Prize, a 2022 Joan Mitchell Fellow, a 2021 Creative Capital Awardee and a 2019 Kindle Project Makers Muse Award recipient.

Andrea Aliseda is a food and culture writer and vegan recipe developer and dog mom based in Brooklyn, NY currently working on her debut plant-based Mexican cookbook. Find her on instagram at @andrea__aliseda and Substack at: andreaaliseda.substack.com.

Bill McKibben is an author, educator, and environmentalist, who helped found 350.org, the first global grassroots climate campaign, and who has recently helped found Third Act an organization that builds a progressive organizing movement for people over the age of 60.

Bread and Puppet Press prints images chiseled in masonite by Peter Schumann, founder and director of the Bread and Puppet Theater. The press, founded by Elka Schumann makes all the hand-printed and painted items for sale and produces printed work for theater performances. Our emphasis is on utilitarian uses of art, for such vital activities as celebration, decoration, information, argumentation, rumination and puppetry!

Carla J Simmons holds an associates degree in Positive Human Development and Social Change. She works to embody the responsibilities of this degree through art and journalism, while representing her community in the most authentic way possible.

Chloë Boxer writes fiction and makes television. She has stories in Joyland, DIAGRAM, and The Michigan Quarterly Review.

Chris Lloyd (b. 1994, Albuquerque, NM) is a multimedia artist based in Brooklyn, NY. "In Solitude Until The End of Time" presents Lloyd's largest-scale works to date. Layers of tactility expand across works that are suspended in shadow boxes and hung as 'scrolls' along the walls. His practice builds in watercolor, sewing, architectural pin-plotting, laser engraving and collage, imbuing personal narrative and storytelling in his constructions. Recent shows include 'Two Birds, One Stone', Gern En Regalia, 2020, and a subsequent solo booth at NADA NY with the same in 2022. Recent group shows include 'At the Center Of My Ironic Faith', Cassandra Cassandra, Toronto, Canada 2021, 'Everyday Secrets,' Luce Gallery, Torino, Italy, 2021 and 'The Swamp Show, Mundus Press, Northern Massachusetts, 2021.

Dyani White Hawk (b. 1976, Sičáŋǧu Lakota) is a multidisciplinary artist based in Minneapolis. Her practice, strongly rooted in painting and beadwork, extends into sculpture, installation, video and performance, reflecting upon cross-cultural experiences through the amalgamation of influences from Lakota and Euro/American abstraction. White Hawk was featured in the 2022 Whitney Biennial and recent solo exhibitions at the Museum of Contemporary Art Denver and Kemper Museum of Contemporary Art. Recent awards include Anonymous Was a Woman, Academy of Arts and Letters, United States Artists, and others.

Dylan Smith's work appears in Vol. 1 Brooklyn, Chestnut Review, Bending Genres, and other literary places on the internet. He also reads fiction submissions for X-R-A-Y Lit, writes a monthly fiction column for Farewell Transmission, and plants flowers on rooftops in Brooklyn for money. Find him on Twitter @ dylan_a_smith

Daniel Barreto Born 1991 is an artist based in México City who has a diverse range of creative talents including animation, film, visuals, murals, music, and design. In 2016, Daniel received his BFA from the School of the Museum of Fine Arts/TUFTS in Boston.

Esther Elia (she/her) received a BFA in Illustration from California College of the Arts, and an MFA in Painting/Drawing from the University of New Mexico. Her art practice focuses on the Assyrian experience in diaspora, and uses painting and sculpture to explore themes of creating homeland and culture as a currently stateless nation. She uses storytelling as a tool for decolonization and community healing, and collects contemporary Assyrian histories as a salve to the Western institutional canon and its hyper-focus of Assyrians solely within their ancient context.

Food with Fam is a community built on reciprocity and reimagining our relationship to food and one another. Since our birth at the dawn of the COVID-19 pandemic, we have aimed to build a sustainable model of produce distributions and culinary programming that not only provides nourishment and sustenance to disadvantaged neighborhoods throughout New York City, but creates long-lasting trust and connections that can become a vehicle for greater health and collaboration amongst New Yorkers.

Francesca DiMattio makes sculpture inspired by the domestic. Looking at the history of porcelain, she shifts how we are used to seeing the decorative. Polite and sweet designs become rogue and powerful. She collapses time and space making new hybrids that question fixed notions of beauty, femininity and cultural hierarchies.

Hangama Amiri holds an MFA from Yale University where she graduated in 2020 from the Painting and Printmaking Department. She received her BFA from NSCAD University in Halifax, Nova Scotia, and is a Canadian Fulbright and Post-Graduate Fellow at Yale University School of Art and Sciences (2015-2016). Amiri works predominantly in textiles to examine notions of home, as well as how gender, social norms, and larger geopolitical conflict impact the daily lives of women, both in Afghanistan and in the diaspora.

Hannah Beerman is a person and a painter and keeps learning things the hard way. She was born in 1992 in Nyack, NY and as of this printing, does not believe in ghosts. She went to Bard for her BA and Hunter for MFA

Jennifer Givhan is a Mexican-American and Indigenous poet and novelist from the Southwestern desert and the recipient of poetry fellowships from the National Endowment for the Arts and PEN/Rosenthal Emerging Voices. The author of five full-length poetry collections, her latest novel RIVER WOMAN, RIVER DEMON was chosen for Amazon's Book Club and as a National Together We Read Library Pick, and was featured on CBS Morning. Her novel TRINITY SIGHT won the Southwest Book Award.

Jessie Kindig is the editor of Vole Prochaine, a zine of writing by animals for animals.

Jumana Manna is a visual artist and filmmaker. Her work explores how power is articulated, focusing on the body, land and materiality in relation to colonial inheritances and histories of place. Jumana was raised in Jerusalem and lives in Berlin.

Kirk Gordon is a designer, landscape architect, and tallgrass prairie native with a background in zoology and plant biology. He is currently based in Brooklyn, where he can be found hoarding native plants in his backyard.

Keegan Dakkar Lomanto is a Multi-Disciplinary Artist, Born in New York City, 1990

Lily Consuelo Saporta Tagiuri is an industrial designer and eco-futurist whose practice is aimed at public engagement, ecological equity, and joy. Her work addresses emerging climates and conditions of cities specifically pertaining to clean water, food sovereignty, fresh air, and green space. Through the construction of ecosystemic tools, material experimentation, collaborations, and installations, she responds to the ecological circumstances we are collectively contending with.

Philip Poon is a registered architect based in New York City. His practice explores the contemporary American condition, in particular the architectural and spatial expressions of the Asian-American experience.

Sophia Giovannitti is an artist and author who lives in New York.

Tania Willard of Secwepemc Nation and settler heritage, is an artist, curator, and assistant professor in visual arts at UBC Okanagan, Syilx territories. Her work as a curator and artist has been shown nationally with curated exhibitions of note at Vancouver Art Gallery, Beat Nation: Art Hip Hop and Aboriginal Culture, the Museum of Anthropology UBC, Unceded Territories: Lawrence Paul Yuxweluptun, and Landmarks 2017 in National Parks across Turtle Island. Willard's ongoing collaborative project BUSH gallery is a land-based gallery grounded in Indigenous knowledges in her home territories of Secwepemcúlecw.

Tyrrell Tapaha is a 6th generation Diné weaver and sheepherder based in the Four Corners.

Veladya Chapman is an herbalist, living and homesteading in rural Georgia with her partner, Matt and 3 year old daughter, Aura. Amongst herbalism, Veladya studies and teaches breathwork, entheogens, womb wisdom and holistic nutrition. Her heart is expanded by guiding others towards elevated ways of being.

Who Tattoo AKA Joji Sanabria is a queer Puerto Rican tattoo artist based in San Francisco, Ca. His style of tattooing is acid traditional; often colorful, weird, playful and cute.

Yaku Pérez Guartambel is a Kichwa-Kañari lawyer, scholar and water defender. He has spent the last three decades defending indigenous rights to self-determination and water systems in the Andean highlands of Ecuador. Yaku, who authored eight books, has been criminalized for defending water, tortured, jailed and a victim of assassination attempts. In 2018 he was elected governor of the province of Azuay, and in 2021/2023 he ran for presidential office.

Image Index

January
Amaryllis R. Flowers

What Haunts Us / What Heals Us

2020, gouache and color pencil on paper.

57 x 90 in.

March
Bread and Puppet Press

Not Alone

woodcut, ink on fabric.

April
Alfredo Jaar

Be Afraid of the Enormity of the Possible

2015, Neon.

May
Francesca DiMattio

Meissen Pump

2022, Glaze on porcelain with stoneware tile pedestal.

27.5x17x11 in.

Courtesy the artist and Nina Johnson, Miami

Photos by Adam Reich with the exception of Meissen Pump by Karen Pearson.

June
Esther Elia

Bodybuilder Deities in the Garden

2022, Acrylic on Canvas.

69x59 in.

July
10th Floor Studio

Boombox

August
Tyrrell Tapaha

Carrizo Mountain Dance

2021, Diné-style tapestry, commercial and handspun vegetal-dyed Navajo Churro yarn.

16x35 in.

September
Hannah Beerman

Weightlifter3

2022, Acrylic, dried flowers, Polaroid, gouache, and chip clip on board.

10x10 in.

Keegan Dakkar Lomanto

Sunflower

2018, graphite, ink, colored pencil, correction fluid, bodily fluid on paper.

October
Dyani White Hawk

Untitled (Blue and Gold)

2016, acrylic, oil, vintage beads, thread on canvas.

20 x 20 in.

November
Chris Lloyd

The Shadow of Night Makes Way for Morning Light

December
Hangama Amiri

Mehmana/Guests

2022, Chiffon, muslin, cotton, polyester, silk, velvet, vinyl, ikat-print, suede, and found fabric.

62 × 83 in.

Photography credit: Chris Gardner